MadCap Flare
certified test review + developer's guide
Scott DeLoach

Copyright © 2010 by Scott DeLoach

834 C Dekalb Ave
Atlanta, GA 30307

www.clickstart.net

Designer: Patrick Hofmann

Developed in MadCap Flare

ISBN: 978-0-578-00117-3

9 8 7 6

Printed and bound in the United States of America

Dedication

This book is dedicated to my mother, Sylvia Jo DeLoach.
Thanks, mom, for always believing in me.

Contents

Topics 45

Creating topics 47

Formatting and design 155

Single sourcing 191

Publishing 209

Feedback 247

Source control 251

Appendices 263

Additional resources 265

Keyboard shortcuts (by task) 267

Keyboard shortcuts (by key) 272

Guide to Flare files 277

Quick task index 281

Introduction

This book was designed to be both a study guide for the certified MAD program and a comprehensive guide for Flare users. It meets the needs of a wide range of Flare users, including those who are:

- New to content development, help authoring, and technical writing

- Transitioning from RoboHelp or another help authoring tool

- Transitioning from Word

- Transitioning from FrameMaker

- Upgrading from a previous version

- Looking for a quick 'refresher' of key features

- Preparing to be Certified MAD for Flare™

This book provides the essential information you need to use all of Flare's major features. It also includes information that will appeal to advanced users, such as keyboard shortcuts, Flare file descriptions, and a quick task index.

What is 'Certified MAD for Flare?'

The certified MadCap Advanced Developer (MAD) program recognizes and validates your ability to use MadCap products. Being certified MAD for Flare is the best way to demonstrate your abilities and stay up to date with MadCap Flare. It also sounds cool!

To be certified MAD for Flare, you will need to:

□ pass the certification test

□ submit a sample Flare project

About the exam

The certification test is a 75 minute, 50 question test that you take on the Web. The passing score is 70%. The test is not easy—you will need to study and review this book's sample questions to pass. We designed the certification program to be a true assessment of Flare users' advanced abilities, and we want those who pass to be proud to be Certified MAD for Flare!

About the sample project

The sample project is a Flare project that demonstrates your ability to use Flare. The project does not have a time limit, and you can choose the subject.

Preparing for certification

The best way to prepare for the certification test is to take a Flare class. The questions on the test are drawn directly from the course guides and class content. You will also learn best practices for creating Flare projects, which will help you successfully pass the sample project requirements.

This guide is also a great way to prepare for certification, and it is designed to complement the training classes. The questions at the end of each chapter are similar to the test questions, and they can be used to review Flare features before taking the test. The step-by-step instructions will help you successfully create the sample project.

Icons used in this guide

The following icons are used throughout this guide to help you find important and time-saving information.

Icon	Meaning	Description
⚠	Caution	Important advice that could cause data loss or unnecessary aggravation if not followed.
NEW!	New Feature	A new or substantially enhanced feature in Flare 6.
◇	Note	Additional information about a topic.
TIP▷	Tip	A recommended best practice, shortcut, or workaround.

Updates

For the most up-to-date information about this book, see **www.clickstart.net**.

For the most up-to-date information about Flare, see MadCap Software's website at **www.madcapsoftware.com** and the Flare forums at **forums.madcapsoftware.com**.

What's new in Flare 6

Flare 6 includes over 50 user-requested enhancements. The major new features are listed in the table below.

Feature	See Page(s)
HTML, XHTML and XML file import (new process)	66
Video import (new process and more formats)	84
Sound import	85
Link Viewer	97
TOC issues – find and fix	126
WebHelp mobile	186
PDF advanced options	217
Batch generate	221
Topic templates (improved process)	237
File tags	238
Reports	240
Multiple topic reviews	244
Source control merge changes	260

Six reasons to use Flare

Flare is an advanced XML-based content authoring application with powerful single sourcing features. In addition to its innovative user interface and excellent online help, Flare has many strengths that make it a great choice for developing online help, policies and procedures, knowledge bases, user guides, and technical manuals. This section lists six reasons why I use Flare and recommend it to clients.

XML-based architecture and clean code

Flare's XML-based architecture allows MadCap to support multiple XML schemas such as XHTML and DITA and potentially add support for additonal schemas such as DocBook in the future. All of Flare's project files are XML-based, so they're extremely small and easy to read in Notepad or an XML editor.

Flare's XML-based authoring also means that it produces clean code.

Content linking

Flare allows you to import content from Microsoft Word, Adobe FrameMaker, HTML, XHTML, and DITA documents and other Flare projects. When you import content, you can link the imported topics to the source document or Flare project.

Content linking allows you to maintain your content in different applications and reuse it in Flare. For example, anyone within your company can develop content in Word, and you can import their content into your Flare project. If you have multiple Flare projects, you can link common formatting elements such as stylesheets and page layouts and reuse them.

Page layouts

Page layouts can be used to set the page size and margins and to set up headers and footers for print targets. Flare's page layouts are very advanced: you can set up different headers and footers for title, first, empty, odd, and even pages, and you can create and use multiple page layouts. For example, you can use a landscape page layout for wide topics and a two-column page layout for your index.

Snippets

Snippets can be used to reuse any content, including text, images, and tables in multiple topics. You can use snippets to reuse a note, a procedure, or even a screenshot and its description.

Source control support

Because Flare has an open XML architecture, Flare projects are compatible with most source control applications, including CVS, Subversion, Microsoft Visual SourceSafe (VSS), and Microsoft Team Foundation Server (TFS). Flare provides integrated support for VSS and TFS, which means you can check files in or out and perform other source control tasks from within Flare. You can even set up Flare to automatically send an email or instant message to another team member if you need to check out a file they have open.

Table styles

In other help authoring tools and HTML editors, you must use inline formatting to format tables. If you need to change the table formatting, it's usually very tedious and time consuming.

In Flare, you can use table styles to specify table borders, background colors, captions, and other properties. You can even format header and footer rows and set up alternating background colors for rows and columns. Flare allows you to create multiple table styles, so you can create online- and print-specific table styles.

Projects

This section covers:

- Creating a new project
- Converting from RoboHelp
- Converting from FrameMaker
- Converting from DITA

New projects

Project files have a .flprj extension (for 'Flare project'). Flare's project file is a small XML file—feel free to open it in Notepad and take a look.

The project file is stored in your project's top-level folder. You name this folder when you create a new project. For example, if your project is named 'MyFirstProject,' your top-level folder is named 'MyFirstProject.' By default, Flare creates your top-level folder in the My Documents\My Projects folder.

In addition to the project file, your top-level folder contains four subfolders: Analyzer, Content, Project, and Output.

The **Analyzer** folder contains data for the Analyzer reports, such as broken links and topics that are not in a TOC or index.

The **Content** folder contains all of your topics, images, sounds, stylesheets, and movies.

The **Project** folder contains your conditional tag sets, context-sensitive help map files, glossaries, skins, TOCs, and variable sets. Wondering where the index file is? There's not one—Flare stores your index keywords in your topics.

The **Output** folder contains your generated targets, like HTML Help or print documents.

'What languages does Flare support?'

Flare provides full support for the following languages:

□ Danish	□ French	□ Portuguese
□ Dutch	□ German	□ Spanish
□ English	□ Italian	□ Swedish
□ Finnish	□ Norwegian	□ Thai

Flare supports Unicode, so you can write your topics in any language. Flare also includes translated WebHelp skins for the languages listed above and for numerous region-specific languages.

The Flare interface can be viewed in English, French, German, or Japanese. You can change the language in the Select UI Language dialog box when you open Flare. If the dialog box does not appear, you can turn it on by selecting **Tools > Options** and selecting the **Show Select UI Language Dialog on Startup** option.

Creating a new project

You can create a new project using a template. In fact, you use templates to create everything in Flare, including topics, stylesheets, glossaries, skins, and variable sets. Project templates allow you to include sample topics when you create a new project. For example, Flare includes a project template named 'Application Help Sample.' If you create a project using this template, Flare will create some sample topics for you: 'Contacting,' 'Getting Started,' 'Introduction,' 'Welcome,' and 'What's New.' If you want to create a blank project, you can use the 'Empty' template.

Shortcut	Toolbar	Menu
Alt+F, N		File > New Project

To create a new project:

1 Click 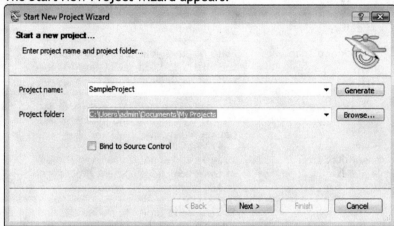 in the toolbar.
   —OR—
   Select **File** > **New Project**.

   The Start New Project wizard appears.

2 Type a **Project Name**.
   You don't have to type the .flprj extension. Flare will add it for
   you if you leave it out.

3 Type or select a **Project Folder** and click **Next**.

4 Select a **Language** and click **Next**.
   The language you select determines which dictionary is used
   for spell checking.

5 Select a **Source** and click **Next**.
   You can select a factory template or your own project
   template.

6 Select an **Available Target** and click **Next**.

7 Select **Create the Project**.

8 Click **Finish**.
   Your new project opens in Flare.

Converting from RoboHelp

Flare features that are not in RoboHelp

Flare includes the following features that are not found in RoboHelp 8:

Feature	Description	See page(s)
Block and span bars	Flare displays your tags in block and span bars. You can select tags to move, sort, or modify content.	51
Project linking	You can share any Flare file (such as topics, stylesheets, and masterpages) between projects.	68
Annotations	You can add annotations to your topics to track your development progress or to add comments for co-authors.	243
Topic reviews	You can send topics to reviewers, and they can annotate or modify your topics without using Flare.	244
Toggler links	Toggler links are similar to drop-down links, but they can be used to open or close multiple blocks of content.	105
Relationship links	Relationship links are similar to help controls, but they can be used to group links based on topic types.	112
DotNet Help format	DotNet Help is MadCap's help format for .NET applications. Unlike HTML Help, it can run from a file server.	211
DITA and XPS export	Flare can create DITA and XPS documents.	211
FrameMaker export	You can single-source your content by exporting to FrameMaker to create print documents.	217

RoboHelp features that are not in Flare

RoboHelp 8 includes the following features that are not in Flare 6:

Feature	What You Should Do
FlashHelp	Use WebHelp.
	MadCap has announced that they may release a Flash-based help format. See 'What about FlashHelp?' on page 211 for more information.
Forms	Use another HTML editor to create and edit forms.
	To open a topic in another HTML editor, right-click the topic and select **Open with** > *your HTML editor*.
JavaHelp	Use DotNet Help or WebHelp.
	If you cannot use DotNet Help or WebHelp, contact MadCap Software and ask them to add support for JavaHelp. The MadCap team is very interested in user feedback. If they see enough interest, they may add support for JavaHelp.
Oracle Help	Consider using DotNet Help or WebHelp.
	If you can't use either of these formats, ask MadCap to add support for Oracle Help. They may add an Oracle Help target type if enough users are interested.
PDF import	Save the PDF document as HTML and import the HTML file.
RoboSource Control	Use any source control program, including RoboSource Control if you have been using it.
	If you use Microsoft Visual SourceSafe or Team Foundation Server, Flare provides the same integrated features RoboHelp provides with RoboSource Control.
What's This Help? Composer	Use Flare's Alias Editor to create context-sensitive help.

Top ten RoboHelp conversion 'gotchas'

RoboHelp and Flare are similar, but there are some features that are *just* different enough to be confusing. There are also a few Flare features that can be hard to find, especially if you are accustomed to using RoboHelp.

Here's my list of the top ten features that I had trouble understanding, finding, and remembering how to use when I started using Flare.

10 Viewing the XHTML Code

Flare makes it a little tricky to view your code. You can open a 'pseudo code' editor by clicking the <t> ▾ icon in the XML Editor toolbar, or you can open a full-featured code editor by clicking 🖳 .

9 Using condition tag boxes

Flare's Content Explorer provides condition tag boxes to identify topics that use condition tags. Unfortunately, an empty condition tag box looks like a checkbox. I tried to select these boxes for a few days and thought they must be broken. According to the Flare help community, many other users assume they are checkboxes too.

8 Indexing

Indexing is very different in Flare than in RoboHelp. Although Flare does not include an indexing wizard, you can create an 'auto-index phrase set' to automatically add keywords to your topics.

7 Auto-generating a TOC

In RoboHelp, you can auto-generate a TOC based on your Project Manager tab. Folders on the Project tab become books, and topics become pages. If you change the organization on the Project tab, you have to regenerate the TOC or update it yourself.

In Flare, you can auto-generate a TOC book to automatically create links to headings inside a topic. If you add or remove headings in the topic, the TOC is automatically updated.

6 Using templates

In RoboHelp 7 and earlier, a template is used to format topics and include boilerplate content, such as a logo or a header and footer. The headers and footers are dynamically linked to topics. If you change a template's header or footer, topics that use the template are automatically updated.

In Flare, everything (including stylesheets, snippets, tables, topics, and TOCs), uses a template. You can use a template to include boilerplate content and formatting, but it is not dynamically linked to the item you created. If you update a template, the items you created using the template are not updated. However, Flare's master pages *do* allow you to dynamically update topics.

5 Using master pages

In RoboHelp 8, templates were renamed master pages. RoboHelp 8's master pages are similar to Flare's master pages, but Flare's master pages provide more features.

4 Using page layouts

Flare's page layouts can be used to set the page size, page margins, headers and footers for print documents. RoboHelp automatically sets most of these options, but you cannot change them.

3 Viewing RoboHelp's WebHelp vs Flare's WebHelp

RoboHelp's WebHelp and Flare's WebHelp have very different default designs (see page 211 to compare screenshots).

2 Viewing browse sequences

In RoboHelp, browse sequences appear as either a graphical bar at the top of your topics (HTML Help) or as small arrows in the navigation pane (WebHelp). RoboHelp's HTML Help browse sequences require the HHActiveX.dll file to be installed on the user's computer.

In Flare, browse sequences appear as either a TOC item (HTML Help) or as an accordion item (DotNet Help and WebHelp). Because they do not appear on a custom tab, Flare's HTML Help browse sequences do not require a .dll file.

You can add browse sequence next and previous buttons to your WebHelp toolbar using the Skin Editor. For more information, see 'Using a browse sequence' on page 150.

1 **Context-sensitive help paths**

Flare organizes your generated WebHelp topics in a "Content" folder. Since RoboHelp does not use a Content folder, your context-sensitive help links might not work after you convert to Flare. If you cannot change the code to include the Content folder, you can remove it from your WebHelp files by selecting "Do not use 'Content' folder in output" on the Advanced tab in your WebHelp target.

Importing a RoboHelp project

You can import projects created with RoboHelp X5 or later (.xpj files), RoboHelp X4 or earlier (.mpj files), or other help authoring tools (.hhp files).

Shortcut	Toolbar	Menu
Alt+F, I, M	None	File > Import Project

To import a RoboHelp project:

1 Select **File** > **Import Project** > **Import (Non-Flare) Project**. The Import Project Wizard appears.

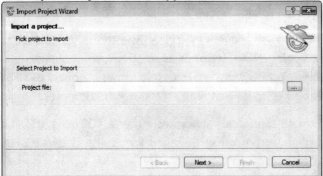

2 Click [...] to find a project file to import.
The Open dialog box appears.

3 Locate and select a project file.

- RoboHelp X5 or later: .xpj file

- RoboHelp X4 or earlier: .mpj file

- Other tools: .hhp file

4 Click **Open**.

5 Click **Next**.

6 Type a **Project Name**.

7 Type or select a **Project Folder** and click **Next**.

8 Select whether you want to **Convert all topics at once**.
This option converts your topic files from HTML to XHTML. If you don't select this option, your files will remain as HTML files and your index terms will not be imported.

9 Select whether you want to **Convert inline formatting to CSS styles**.
If your project uses inline formatting, you should convert the inline formatting to styles. Styles are much easier to create and maintain.

10 Click Next.

11 Select a **Language** for spell checking and click **Finish**.
The RoboHelp project is imported into Flare. Your new Flare project file will have a .flprj extension.

'What happens to my... ?'

The following table explains how RoboHelp's features convert to Flare.

RoboHelp Feature	Converts?	Comments
Browse sequences	✓	
Conditional tags	✓	Stored in a condition tag set named 'Primary.'
Custom colors		You must recreate the colors in Flare.
Dictionaries		See 'Where's my dictionary?' on page 31.
HTML topics	✓	Converted to XHTML either when imported (recommended) or when opened.
Folders	✓	
Forms	✓	Forms are converted, but you cannot edit or create forms in Flare. To edit a form, right-click its topic and select **Open with** > *your HTML editor*.
Frames	✓	Frames are converted, but you cannot edit or create forms in Flare. To edit a frame, right-click its topic and select **Open with** > *your HTML editor*.
Glossary	✓	
Inline formatting	✓	Maintained, or can be converted to styles.
Publishing locations	✓	Converted to 'Publishing destinations.'
Single-Source layouts	✓	Converted to 'Targets.'
Snippets	✓	
Sounds	✓	
Table of contents	✓	
Template headers and footers	✓	Converted to snippets.

RoboHelp Feature	Converts?	Comments
Movies	✓	
Variables	✓	Stored in a variable set named 'Primary.'
WebHelp skins		See 'Where are my WebHelp skins?' on page 32.
Windows	✓	Converted to skins.

'Where is my dictionary?' ⏵

RoboHelp dictionaries are not imported, but you *can* add your dictionary terms to Flare.

To add your dictionary terms in Flare:

1 In Windows Explorer, open the C:\Program Files\MadCap Software\MadCap Flare\Flare.app\Resources\SSCE folder.

2 Find your dictionary.
Dictionary file names are based on their language. For example, Flare's 'English - American' dictionary is named 'ssce**am**.tlx.'

3 Just to be safe, make a backup copy of your Flare dictionary.

4 Locate your RoboHelp dictionary.
To find your dictionary:

◻ Open RoboHelp HTML.

◻ Select **Tools** > **Spelling Options**.

◻ Select the **Dictionary** tab. Your 'dictionaries' paths are listed in the Path column.

5 Open your RoboHelp dictionary in Notepad.

6 Copy all of your terms and close your RoboHelp dictionary.

7 Open your Flare dictionary in Notepad.

8 Paste your terms at the end of the file.

9 Save your new Flare dictionary.

'Where are my WebHelp skins?'

RoboHelp skins are imported into Flare, but they are not set up. You can use Flare's Skin Editor to set up your skins. See 'Modying a skin' on page 182.

Converting from FrameMaker

Top ten FrameMaker conversion 'gotchas'

Flare and FrameMaker have very different interfaces. However, both applications can be used to create print documents. When FrameMaker is combined with Quadralay's WebWorks ePublisher, you can use it or Flare to create online formats such as HTML Help.

If you focus on tasks and features, FrameMaker and Flare are similar applications. It takes time to learn the Flare interface when you transition, just as it takes time to learn FrameMaker. I've created a list of the top ten differences between FrameMaker and Flare to hopefully make the transition easier for you.

10 Keyboard shortcuts

Like FrameMaker, Flare provides extensive keyboard shortcuts (see page 267 for a list). However, Flare uses 'Alt' key shortcuts rather than 'Esc' key shortcuts.

9 Importing content

You can import content into a FrameMaker document, or you can copy and paste content into FrameMaker. In Flare, you can import content into your project to create new topics. If you want to import content into a topic, you can copy and paste.

8 Inserting graphics

In FrameMaker, images are placed inside anchored or unanchored frames. Placing an image in an anchored frame allows the image to 'move' with the surrounding text. Placing an image inside an unanchored frame fixes its position on the page.

In Flare, images automatically 'move' with the surrounding text. If you place an image inside a div tag, you can fix its position.

7 Cross references and hyperlinks

If you import a FrameMaker document that contains cross references, the cross references convert to Flare cross references. In Flare, you can use hyperlinks or cross references to link to other topics. Most Flare users use hyperlinks instead of cross references, especially since hyperlinks can also link to websites and PDF documents. You can keep using cross references to link to topics, but you will need to use hyperlinks to link to websites and PDF documents.

6 Master pages

In FrameMaker, a master page is used to specify the page layout. In Flare, a master page is used to add content to topics in online targets. For example, a Flare master page can be used to add a copyright statement to the bottom of every topic in HTML Help. You can also use master pages for print targets in Flare, but page layouts offer many more options than master pages.

5 Templates and page layouts

A FrameMaker template contains master pages that specify the formatting, header, and footer for different types of pages (for example, title, odd, and even pages). In Flare, a page layout contains pages that are used to format difference types of pages.

4 Lists

In FrameMaker, bulleted and numbered lists are paragraph styles. When you import a FrameMaker document, list styles become paragraph styles, just like in FrameMaker. However, lists can also be created in Flare using the ul ('unordered' or bulleted) list and ol ('ordered' or numbered) list tags rather than the paragraph tag. You can create lists using either method, but it might be confusing to use both approaches in the same project.

3 'Missing' .book files?

Flare does not use .book files. When you import a FrameMaker .book file, Flare will import all of the included .fm files and create a table of contents (TOC) based on your FrameMaker 'TOC' file.

2 Styles

Flare uses styles to format your content. Styles are stored in stylesheets and are basically a combination of the paragraph and character designers in FrameMaker. When you import a FrameMaker document, Flare can create a stylesheet that includes all of your FrameMaker character and paragraph styles. Table styles can also be converted into table-specific stylesheets.

1 Topic-based authoring

In Flare, your content is separated into short (usually 1-4 printed pages) topics rather than long chapter or section documents. It seems weird and unnecessary at first—why do you need so many small topics? The reason small topics are useful is the same reason multiple chapter documents are useful: it's easier to work with focused 'chunks' of content.

In Flare, topics are organized into folders in the Content Explorer and books in the table of contents (TOC). The folders and book are similar to your chapters, and the TOC itself is similar to a FrameMaker .book file. You can easily move topics around in a TOC book, just as you can move .fm chapter documents in a FrameMaker book. You can also easily add new topics to a TOC book. Topic-based authoring also makes it very easy to reuse content in multiple topics. For example, you can reuse a 'copyright' or 'Conventions in this guide' topic in multiple Flare projects.

Importing a FrameMaker document

When you import a FrameMaker document, you can divide the document into smaller topics based on styles that are used in your FrameMaker document. For example, you can create a new topic for each 'Heading 1' in the document.

Flare can create a stylesheet (.css file) based on the formatting in your FrameMaker document. Or, you can apply an existing stylesheet to reformat your imported topics to match your other topics.

Creating a new project based on a FrameMaker document

You can create a new project based on a FrameMaker document. If you want to import a FrameMaker document into an existing project, see 'Importing a FrameMaker document' on page 38.

Shortcut	Toolbar	Menu
Alt+F, I, P	none	File > Import Project > Import FrameMaker Documents

To create a new project based on a FrameMaker document:

1 Select **File** > **Import Project** > **Import FrameMaker Documents**.
   The Import FrameMaker wizard appears.

2 Click **Next**.
   When you import a FrameMaker document, Flare saves your settings in an import data file (these files have a .flimpfm extension). You can reuse these settings when you re-import the FrameMaker document or import similar documents.

3 Click **Add Files**.

4 Select a .fm or .book FrameMaker file and click **Open**.
If needed, you can select more than one FrameMaker
document.

5 If you plan to continue editing the file in FrameMaker, select
Link generated files to source files.

◇ *This option is also called 'Easy Sync.' It allows you to link
the imported topics to the FrameMaker document. When you
re-import the document, Flare replaces the original topics
with the new topics.*

*Linked topics have a chain (⅜) icon on their tab in the XML
Editor.*

6 Click **Next**.

7 Type a **Project Name**.

8 Type or select a **Project Folder**.

9 Click **Next**.

10 Select a style or styles to use to create new topics.
For example, you can create a new topic for each Heading 1 in
the FrameMaker document.

11 Click **Next**.

12 Select whether you want to create new topics based on the
length of your FrameMaker document. If you decide to create
new topics, you can also automatically add links to the previous
and next topics.

13 Click **Next**.

14 Select a stylesheet for the new topic(s).
If you select a stylesheet, Flare will apply the stylesheet to
your topics and automatically 'map' styles with matching
names. For example 'Heading 1' in FrameMaker will become
'h1' in Flare. If you do not select a stylesheet, Flare will create
a stylesheet based on the formatting in your FrameMaker
document.

15 Click **Next**.

16 Map (or 'match') your FrameMaker paragraph-level styles to your stylesheet's (.css) styles.
For example, if you use a style named "HeadText1" in FrameMaker, map it to "h1." Styles will map to the "p" (paragraph) style by default.

17 Click **Next**.

18 If needed, map your character-level styles, like bold, to Flare styles.
Character-level styles will map to the "span" tag by default.

19 Click **Next**.

20 If needed, map your cross-reference (x-ref) styles to Flare styles.
Cross reference-styles will map to the MadCap|xref style by default.

21 Click **Finish**.

Importing a FrameMaker document into a project

You can import a FrameMaker document into an existing Flare project and divide it into multiple topics.

Shortcut	Toolbar	Menu
Alt+P, I D	none	Project > Import File > Add FrameMaker Import File

To import a FrameMaker document:

1 Open the Project Organizer.

2 Right-click the **Imports** folder and select **Add FrameMaker Import File**.

The Add FrameMaker Import File dialog box appears.

3 Select a **Source** template.

4 Type a **File Name**.

5 Click **Add**.

6 Click **OK**.
    The Frame Import Editor appears.

7 Click **Add Files**.
    The Open dialog box appears.

8 Select a .fm or .book FrameMaker document and click **Open**.
    If needed, you can select more than one FrameMaker
    document.

9 If you plan to continue editing the file in FrameMaker, select
    Link generated files to source files.

   ✐ *This option is also called 'Easy Sync.' It allows you to link
   the imported topics to the FrameMaker document. When you
   re-import the document, Flare replaces the original topics
   with the new topics.*

Linked topics have a chain (🔗) icon on their tab in the XML Editor.

10 Select the **New Topic Styles** tab.

11 Select a style or styles to use to create new topics.
For example, you can create a new topic for each Heading 1 in the FrameMaker document.

12 Select the **Options** tab.

13 Select whether you want to create new topics based on the length of your FrameMaker document. If you decide to create new topics, you can also automatically add links to the previous and next topics.

14 If your images have callouts, select **Generate Images for Anchored Frames When Needed**.

15 If you have sized your images in FrameMaker, select **Preserve Image Size**.

16 Select the **Stylesheet** tab.

17 Select a stylesheet for the new topic(s).
If you select a stylesheet, Flare will apply the stylesheet to your topics and automatically 'map' styles with matching names. For example 'Heading 1' in FrameMaker will become 'h1' in Flare. If you do not select a stylesheet, Flare will create a stylesheet based on the formatting in your FrameMaker document.

18 Select the **Paragraph Styles** tab.

19 Map (or 'match') your FrameMaker paragraph-level styles to your stylesheet's (.css) styles.
For example, if you use a style named "HeadText1" in FrameMaker, map it to "h1." Styles will map to the "p" (paragraph) style by default.

20 Select the **Character Styles** tab.

21 If needed, map your FrameMaker character styles to Flare styles.

Character-level styles will map to the "span" tag by default.

22 Select the **Cross-Reference Styles** tab.

23 If needed, map your FrameMaker cross-reference (x-ref) styles to Flare styles.

Cross reference-styles will map to the MadCap|xref style by default.

24 Click **Import** in the toolbar.

The Accept Imported Documents dialog box appears.

25 Click **Accept**.

The imported topic or topics appear in the Content Explorer in a folder named after the FrameMaker import file you used.

'What happens to my... ?'

The following table explains how FrameMaker's features convert to Flare.

FrameMaker Feature	Converts?	Comments
Character styles	✓	Added to a stylesheet. By default, they are associated with the span style tag.
Conditional Tags	✓	Stored in a condition tag set that is named based on your import file.
Cross reference styles	✓	Added to a stylesheet and associated with the MadCap|xref style tag.
Images	✓	Added to a folder in the Content Explorer named after your import file. Images are converted based on your settings in Adobe Distiller.
Index keywords	✓	Maintained and appear with a green background in your topics. You can hide them if needed.
Inline formatting	✓	Maintained. Can also be converted to styles.

FrameMaker Feature	Converts?	Comments
Master pages		You will need to recreate your master page as a page layout in Flare.
Paragraph styles	✓	Added to a stylesheet. By default, they are associated with the p (paragraph) style tag.
Table styles	✓	Converted to table stylesheets.
'TOC' document	✓	Converted to a Flare TOC named after your import file.
Variables	✓	Added to a variable set that is named after your import file.

Sample questions for this section

1 A Flare project file has the following extension:
A) .prj
B) .hhp
C) .htm
D) .flprj

2 Does Flare support Unicode?
A) Yes
B) No

3 Which of the following files can be created based on a template?
A) Topics
B) Stylesheets
C) Snippets
D) All of the above

4 Why should you select 'Link generated files to source files?'
A) To automatically re-import your Word or FrameMaker documents when you build a target.
B) To keep editing your content in Word or FrameMaker.
C) To import your links and cross references.
D) To import images.

5 Which of the following RoboHelp features is imported but not set up?
A) Index
B) TOC
C) Variables
D) Skins

6 Can you import FrameMaker .fm files and .book files into Flare?
A) Yes
B) No

7 Which of the following FrameMaker features cannot be imported?
A) Styles
B) Index keywords
C) Master pages
D) All of them can be imported

Topics

This section covers:

- Creating topics
- Importing Word documents
- Importing FrameMaker documents
- Importing DITA documents
- Importing HTML, XHTML and XML files
- Importing content from Flare projects
- Adding lists
- Adding tables
- Adding images
- Adding multimedia

Creating topics

In Flare, your content is stored in topics. Each topic is a short (usually 1-4 printed pages) XHTML file that can contain formatted text, images, tables, lists, links, variables, snippets, and other types of content.

'What is XHTML?'

According to the W3C, XHTML is the successor to HTML. XHTML files use HTML tags, but they are an XHTML schema and conform to the strict rules of XML. For example, HTML does not require end tags for the <br>, <li>, or <img> tags. In XHTML, all tags must have end tags. So, a break is written in XHTML as <br />. Another difference is that HTML allows upper, lower, or mixed case tags: <BR>, <br>, or <Br>. In XHTML, you must use lowercase tags.

'Do I have to know XML to use Flare?'

Flare has a built-in WYSIWYG ('what-you-see-is-what-you-get') editor called the 'XML Editor.' You don't have to know anything about HTML, XHTML, or XML to use the XML Editor: Flare writes the code for you. If you *do* know how to write XHTML code, you can view the code and change it yourself.

Creating a topic

You can have as many topics in a project as you need. In fact, some Flare projects have over 10,000 topics.

Shortcut	Toolbar	Menu
Ctrl+T	(Content Explorer toolbar)	Project > Add Topic

To create a topic:

1 Click 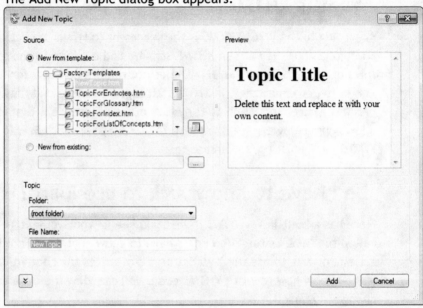 in the Content Explorer toolbar.
—OR—
Select **Project** > **Add Topic**.
—OR—
Press **Ctrl+T**.

The Add New Topic dialog box appears.

2 Select a **Source** template.

3 Select a **Folder** to contain the new topic.

4 Type a **File Name** for the topic.
You don't have to type the .htm extension. Flare will add it for you don't include it.

5 Click **Add**.
The Copy to Project dialog box appears.

6 Click **OK**.
The topic appears in the Content Explorer and opens in the XML Editor.

Viewing your topic titles

In Flare, your topics are listed by their filename in the Content Explorer. However, your users will view your topics by their topic titles in your index and search. Topic titles are also often used in link labels and in the TOC.

By default, your topic titles are set to match the first heading in your topics. You can view and change your topic titles using File List.

To view your topic titles:

1 Select **View** > **File List**.

2 Scroll to the right to the **Title** column.

TIP *You can click the Title column's heading and drag it to the left to make it easier to find.*

Opening a topic

Topics appear in the Content Explorer. When you double-click a topic, it opens as a new tab in the XML Editor. You can open multiple topics at the same time.

Shortcut	Toolbar	Menu
Enter	(Content Explorer toolbar)	none

To open a topic:

1 Select a topic in the Content Explorer.

2 Press **Enter**.
  —OR—
  Click in the Content Explorer toolbar.
  The topic appears as a new tab in the XML Editor.

Opening a topic in the Internal Text Editor

You can open a topic in the Internal Text Editor to view and edit the XHTML code.

To open a topic in the Internal Text Editor:

1 Open the Content Explorer.

2 Right-click a topic and select **Open With > Internal Text Editor**.
The topic opens as a new tab in the Text Editor.

TIP *If the topic is already open in the XML Editor, you can click* 🖳 *to open it in the Internal Text Editor.*

Opening a topic in another editor **TIP**

You can also open topics in other HTML editors—if you know where to look!

To open a topic in another HTML editor:

1 Open the Content Explorer.

2 Right-click a topic and select **Open With > *your HTML editor***.
The topic opens in the HTML editor you selected.

Opening two topics side by side

You can open multiple topics and switch between their tabs, or you can open two topics side by side to compare their content.

To open two topics side by side:

1 Open a topic.
The topic opens as a new tab in the XML Editor.

2 Open another topic.
The second topic opens as a new tab in the XML Editor.

3 Select **Window > Floating**.

The selected topic appears in a small floating window.

4 Click the floating window's title bar and drag the window.

The positioning arrow appears.

5 Drag the window on top of one of the arrows.

The target window location will be shaded light blue.

6 Release your mouse button.

➠ *To move the window back to a tab, select **Window > Floating**, drag the window to the bullseye in the center of the positioning arrow, and release your mouse button.*

Using structure bars in a topic

In Flare, you can use structure bars to view the tagging behind your topics. There are four structure bars: block, span, table column, and table row. The block and table row bars appear on the left side of the XML Editor, and the span and table column bars appear on the top. You can show or hide these bars as needed.

Icon	Description
	Show/hide block bars
	Show/hide span bars
	Show/hide table row bars
	Show/hide table column bars

Inserting special characters

You can insert the following special characters into a topic:

Character	Example		Character	Example
Non-breaking space			N dash	–
Copyright	©		Plus/Minus	±
Registered trademark	®		Greater or equal	≥
Trademark	™		Not equal	≠
Degree	°		Cent	¢
Bullet	•		Euro	€
Double dagger	‡		Pound	£
Ellipses	...		Yen	¥
M dash	—			

TIP *You can also insert a non-breaking space by pressing **Shift+Space**.*

Shortcut	Toolbar	Menu
F11	₋ₐ₋ (XML Editor toolbar)	Insert > Character

To insert a special character:

1 Open a topic.

2 Position your cursor where you want to insert the special character.

3 Click the icon's down arrow.

4 Select a character.

Finding an open topic

If Flare does not have enough room to display each topic's tab, the additional topics appear in a drop-down list.

To find an open topic in the XML Editor:

1 Click the down arrow on the right side of the XML Editor.

2 Select a topic in the drop-down list.

Closing all open topics

When you start using Flare, you will probably forget to close topics. If you have too many topics open, you can close all of them at once.

To close all open topics:

▫ Select **Window** > **Close All Documents**.
All of the open documents close.

To close all open topics except the current topic:

▫ Select **Window** > **Close All Documents Except This One**.
All of the open documents close except the current document.

Deleting a topic

When you delete a topic, Flare moves the topic to the Windows recycle bin. If you need to temporarily remove a topic from your project, you can assign a condition tag to the topic and exclude it from your targets. For more information, see 'Applying a tag to content in a topic' on page 203.

Shortcut	Toolbar	Menu
Delete	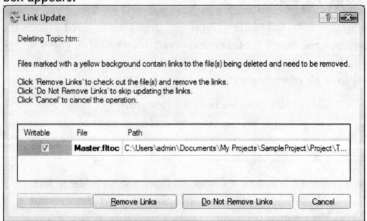	Edit > Delete

To delete a topic:

1   Select the topic in the Content Explorer or File List.

2   Press **Delete**.
    —OR—
    Click ✕.
    The Delete confirmation dialog box appears.

3   Click **OK**.

4   If topics or TOC items link to the topic, the Link Update dialog box appears.

5   Click **Remove Links**.
    The topic is moved to the recycle bin.

Importing Word documents

When you import a Word document, you can divide the document into smaller topics based on styles that are used in your Word document. For example, you can create a new topic for each 'Heading 1' in the document.

Flare can convert your Word template (.dot file) into a stylesheet (.css file) so your formatting stays the same. Or, you can apply an existing stylesheet to reformat your imported topics to match your other topics.

Creating a new project based on a Word document

You can create a new project based on a Word document. If you want to import a Word document into an existing project, see 'Importing a Word document' on page 57.

Shortcut	Toolbar	Menu
Alt+F, I, M	none	File > Import Project > Import MS Word Documents

To create a new project based on a Word document:

1 Select **File** > **Import Project** > **Import MS Word Documents**. The Import Microsoft Word wizard appears.

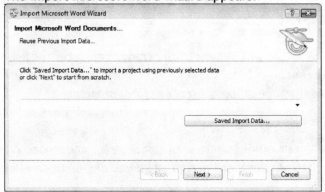

2 Click **Next**.

When you import a Word document, Flare saves your settings in an import data file (these files have a .flimp extension). You can reuse these settings when you re-import the Word document or import similar documents.

3 Click **Add Files**.

4 Select a Word document and click **Open**.

If needed, you can select more than one Word document.

5 If you plan to continue editing the file in Word, select **Link generated files to source files**.

◇ *This option is also called 'Easy Sync.' It allows you to link the imported topics to the Word document. When you re-import the document, Flare replaces the original topics with the new topics.*

Linked topics have a chain (⛓) icon on their tab in the XML Editor.

6 Click **Next**.

7 Type a **Project Name**.

8 Type or select a **Project Folder**.

9 Click **Next**.

10 Select a style or styles to use to create new topics.

For example, you can create a new topic for each Heading 1 in the Word document.

TIP *Flare will automatically create new topics based on manual page breaks in your Word document. You may want to remove manual page breaks before importing.*

11 Click **Next**.

12 Select whether you want to create new topics based on the length of your Word document. If you decide to create new topics, you can also automatically add links to the previous and next topics.

13 Click **Next**.

14 Select a stylesheet for the new topic(s).
If you select a stylesheet, Flare will apply the stylesheet to your topics and automatically 'map' styles with matching names. For example 'Heading 1' in Word will become 'h1' in Flare. If you do not select a stylesheet, Flare will create a stylesheet based on the formatting in your Word document.

15 Click **Next**.

16 Map (or 'match') your Word paragraph-level styles to your stylesheet's (.css) styles.
For example, if you use a style named "HeadText1" in Word, map it to "h1." Styles will map to the "p" (paragraph) style by default.

17 Click **Next**.

18 Map any character-level styles, like bold, to your stylesheet's styles.
Character-level styles will map to the "span" tag by default.

19 Click **Finish**.

Importing a Word document

You can import a Word document into an existing Flare project and divide it into multiple topics.

Shortcut	Toolbar	Menu
Alt+P, I, A	none	Project > Import File > Add MS Word Import File

To import a Word document:

1 Open the Project Organizer.

2 Right-click the **Imports** folder and select **Add MS Word Import File**.

The Add MS Word Import File dialog box appears.

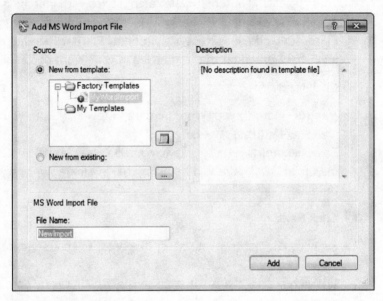

3 Select a **Source** template.

4 Type a **File Name**.

5 Click **Add**.

The MS Word Import Editor appears.

6 Click **Add Files**.

The Open dialog box appears.

7 Select a Word document and click **Open**.

If needed, you can select more than one Word document.

8 If you plan to continue editing the file in Word, select **Link generated files to source files**.

◇ *This option is called 'Easy Sync.' It allows you to link the imported topics to the Word document. When you re-import the document, Flare replaces the original topics with the new topics.*

Linked topics have a chain (⛓) icon on their tab in the XML Editor.

9 Select the **New Topic Styles** tab.

10 Select a style or styles to use to create new topics.
For example, you can create a new topic for each Heading 1 in the Word document.

TIP *Flare will automatically create new topics based on manual page breaks in your Word document. You may want to remove manual page breaks before importing.*

11 Select the **Options** tab.

12 Select whether you want to create new topics based on the length of your Word document. If you decide to create new topics, you can also automatically add links to the previous and next topics.

13 Select the **Stylesheet** tab.

14 Select a stylesheet for the new topic(s).
If you select a stylesheet, Flare will apply the stylesheet to your topics and automatically 'map' styles with matching names. For example 'Heading 1' in Word will become 'h1' in Flare. If you do not select a stylesheet, Flare will create a stylesheet based on the formatting in your Word document.

15 Select the **Paragraph Styles** tab.

16 If needed, map (or 'match') your Word paragraph styles to Flare styles.
For example, if you use a style named "HeadText1" in Word, map it to "h1." Styles will map to the "p" (paragraph) style by default.

17 Select the **Character Styles** tab.

18 If needed, map your Word character-level styles to Flare styles. Character-level styles will map to the "span" tag by default.

19 Click **Import** in the toolbar.
The Accept Imported Documents dialog box appears.

20 Click **Accept**.
The imported topic or topics appear in the Content Explorer in a folder named after the Word import file you used.

Importing DITA documents

You can create a new project based on DITA documents, or you can import DITA documents into an existing Flare project. If you link the imported topics to their source files, you can edit the DITA files and re-import them into your project.

Creating a new project based on a DITA document set

You can create a new project based on a .dita or .ditamap document. If you want to import a DITA document or DITA map into an existing project, see 'Importing a DITA document' on page 64.

Shortcut	Toolbar	Menu
Alt+F, I, O	none	File > Import Project > Import DITA Document Set

To create a new project based on a DITA document set:

1 Select **File** > **Import Project** > **Import DITA Document Set**.
   The Import DITA wizard appears.

2 Click **Next**.
   When you import a DITA document, Flare saves your settings in
   an import data file (these files have a .flimpdita extension).
   You can reuse these settings when you re-import the Word
   document or import similar documents.

3 Click **Add Files**.

4 Select a .dita or .ditamap file and click **Open**.
   If needed, you can select more than one DITA document.

5 If you plan to continue editing the original DITA files, select
   Link generated files to source files.

   ◇ *This option is called 'Easy Sync.' It allows you to link the
   imported topics to the source DITA files. When you re-import
   the document, Flare replaces the original topics with the new
   topics.*

   *Linked topics have a chain (⛓) icon on their tab in the XML
   Editor.*

6 Click **Next**.

7 Type a **Project Name**.

8 Type or select a **Project Folder**.

9 Click **Next**.

10 Select **Import all content files to one folder** if you want to import all of the DITA documents into one folder.

11 Select **'Auto-reimport before Generate Output'** if you want to automatically re-import the DITA document(s) when you generate a target.

12 Select **Preserve ID attributes for elements** if you plan to build a DITA target from your project.

13 Click **Next**.

14 Click **Conversion Styles** if you want to change the formatting of your topics.
Flare will create style classes for your DITA tags. You can modify each tag's formatting later in your stylesheet.

15 Select a stylesheet for the new topic(s).
If you select a stylesheet, Flare will apply the stylesheet to your topics.

16 Click **Finish**.

Importing a DITA document

You can import a .dita or .ditamap document into an existing Flare project.

Shortcut	Toolbar	Menu
Alt+P, I, I	none	Project > Import File > Add DITA Import File

To import a DITA document or DITA map:

1 Open the Project Organizer.

2 Right-click the **Imports** folder and select **Add DITA Import File**. The Add DITA File dialog box appears.

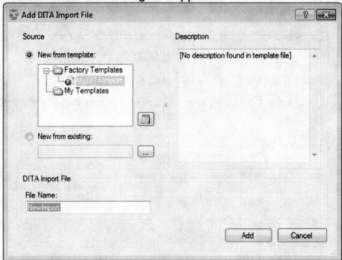

3 Select a **Source** template.

4 Type a **File Name**.

5 Click **Add**.

6 Click **OK**.
The DITA Import Editor appears.

7 Click **Add Files**.

8 Select a .dita or .ditamap document and click **Open**.
If needed, you can select more than one DITA document.

9 If you plan to continue editing the original DITA files, select
Link generated files to source files.

◇ *This option is called 'Easy Sync.' It allows you to link the
imported topics to the source DITA files. When you re-import
the document, Flare replaces the original topics with the new
topics.*

*Linked topics have a chain (⚭) icon on their tab in the XML
Editor.*

10 Select the **Options** tab.

11 Select **Import all content files to one folder** if you want to
import all of the DITA documents into one folder.

12 Select **'Auto-reimport before Generate Output'** if you want to
automatically re-import the DITA document(s) when you
generate a target.

13 Select **Preserve ID attributes for elements** if you plan to build
a DITA target from your project.

14 Select the **Stylesheet** tab.

15 Click **Conversion Styles** if you want to change the formatting
of your topics.
Flare will create style classes for your DITA tags. You can
modify each tag's formatting later in your stylesheet.

16 Select a stylesheet for the new topic(s).
If you select a stylesheet, Flare will apply the stylesheet to
your topics.

17 Click **Import** in the toolbar.
The Accept Imported Documents dialog box appears.

18 Click **Accept**.
The imported topic or topics appear in the Content Explorer in
a folder named after the DITA import file you used.

Importing HTML, XHTML, and XML files NEW!

Any HTML, XHTML, or XML files that are stored in your Content folder automatically appear in your project. Flare will convert HTML files to XHTML when you open them in the XML Editor.

TIP *If you need to import an Acrobat PDF file, save your PDF file as HTML and import the HTML file.*

To import an HTML file:

1   Select **Project** > **Import HTML Files**.
    The **Import HTML Files** wizard appears.

2   Click **Add Files**.

3   Select a .htm, .html, or .xhtml document and click **Open**.
    If needed, you can select more than one document.

4   Click **Next**.

5   Select a folder for the imported topics.

6 Select **Import resources** if you also want to import any files that are used by the selected document(s) (for example, images, stylesheets, or script files used in a topic).

7 Click **Finish**.
The imported topic or topics appear in the Content Explorer in the selected folder.

Importing content from Flare projects

You can link projects to reuse files in multiple projects. For example, you can create a template project that contains your stylesheet, page layout, master page, and a 'Contact Us' topic. When you create a new project, you can link the new project to the template project. If you update the files in the source project, you can re-import them into the shared project.

Flare project import files are stored in the Imports folder in the Project Organizer.

Shortcut	Toolbar	Menu
Alt+P, I, F	none	Project > Import File > Add Flare Project Import File

To import content from another Flare project:

1 Open the Project Organizer.

2 Right-click the **Imports** folder and select **Add Flare Import File**. The Add Flare Import File dialog box appears.

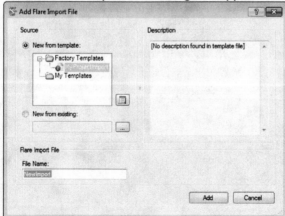

3 Select a **Source** template.

4 Type a **File Name**.

5 Click **Add**.

6 Click **OK**.
The Project Import Editor appears.

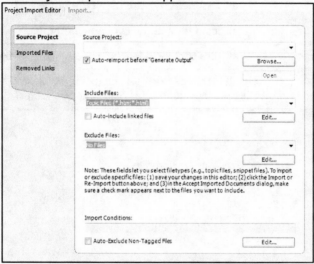

7 Click **Browse** and select a Flare project (.flprj) file.

8 If you want to re-import the shared files when you generate a target, select **Auto-reimport before 'Generate Output.'**

9 For **Include Files**, select the files or file types to be imported.

10 Select **Auto-include linked files** if you also want to import any files that are used by the selected files (for example, images, stylesheets, or script files used in a topic).

11 For **Exclude Files**, select the file types to not be imported.

12 Click **Import**.

TIP *You can include or exclude multiple files or file types. Here are some examples:*

Entry	Description
overview.htm	only the overview.htm topic
*.css	all .css files (stylesheets) in the project
*.css; overview.htm	all .css files and the overview.htm topic
MyCompany	all files that include 'MyCompany' in their filename
.fl	all Flare-specific files (including TOCs, snippets, page layouts, master pages, and variables)

Lists

You can create bulleted lists to help users scan groups of items, or you can create numbered lists to provide step-by-step instructions. Flare provides the following XHTML list types:

Type	Example
Bulleted list	□
Circle bulleted list	○
Square bulleted list	■
Numbered list	1, 2, 3
Lower-alpha numbered list	a, b, c
Upper-alpha numbered list	A, B, C
Lower-roman numbered list	i, ii, iii
Upper-roman numbered list	I, II, III

You can modify the list styles to change the bullet icon or format the bullets or numbers.

Flare provides one toolbar button on the Text Format toolbar for both bulleted and numbered lists. The icon on the button represents the last type of list you created. For example, if you add a bulleted list, the icon will change to a bulleted list.

To view the Text Format toolbar:

□   Click **F** in the XML Editor toolbar.
—OR—
Select **View > Toolbars > Text Formatting**.

Creating a list

You can select the list type when you create the list.

Shortcut	Toolbar	Menu
Alt+O, S	☷ (Text Format toolbar)	Format > List

To create a bulleted or numbered list:

1 Open a topic.

2 Position your cursor where you want to create the list.
   —OR—
   Highlight content that you want to format as a list.

3 Click the ☷ icon's down arrow.

   ◇ *The icon may be a numbered or bulleted list.*

4 Select a list type.

5 If you are creating a new list, type the list items.

Sorting a list

You can use the block bar to sort a list.

To sort a list:

1 Select the list.

2 If you are not viewing tag block bars, click ▤ in the XML Editor's lower toolbar.

3 Right-click the **ol** (numbered list) or **ul** (bulleted list) tag in the block bar.

4 Select **Sort List** to sort the list.
   —OR—
   Select **Reverse List** to sort the list in reverse order.

Tables

You can create tables to organize content and to help users quickly find information. For example, this guide uses tables to present keyboard shortcuts, toolbar buttons, and menu commands.

Tables can contain any type of content, including images and lists, and they can be formatted with background shading and borders. You can have as many table rows or columns as you need, and Flare makes it easy to move, add, and delete columns and rows.

Creating a table

Shortcut	Toolbar	Menu
Alt+A, I, T	none	Table > Insert > Table

To create a table:

1 Open a topic.

2 Position the cursor where you want to create the table.

3 Select **Table** > **Insert** > **Table**.
   The Insert Table dialog box appears.

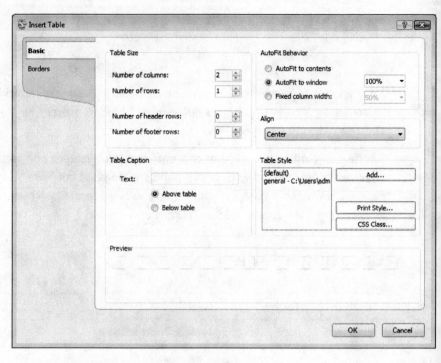

4   Type or select a **Number of Columns**.

5   Type or select a **Number of Rows**.

6   If needed, type or select a number of header and/or footer rows.

7   If needed, type a table caption and select a caption location.

8   Select a column width.

- **AutoFit to Contents** — each column's width is based on the amount of content it contains.

- **AutoFit to Window** — the columns are equally-sized to fit the size of the window.

- **Fixed Column Width** — each column is set to a specified width.

9   Click **OK**.

Creating a table style

In Flare, you can create table styles to format your tables. For example, you can create a table style named 'noBorders' to create tables without borders and another named 'greenHeading' to create tables with a green background for headings.

Table styles are stored in table stylesheets with a .css extension.

Shortcut	Toolbar	Menu
Alt+P, B	none	Project > Add Table Style

To create a table style:

1 Select **Project** > **Add Table Style**.
   The Add New Table Style dialog box appears.

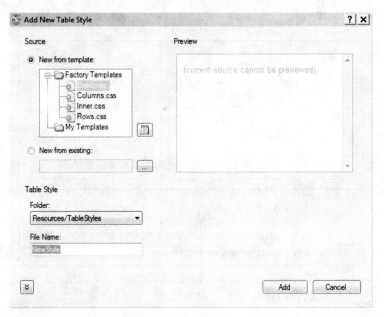

2 Select a **Source** template.

3 Select a **Folder**.
   By default, table stylesheets are stored in the Resources\TableStyles folder.

4 Type a **File Name** for the table stylesheet.

Table stylesheets have a .css extension. If you don't type the extension, Flare will add it for you.

5 Click **Add**.

The Copy to Project dialog box appears.

6 Click **OK**.

The table stylesheet appears in the Content Explorer and opens in the TableStyle Editor.

To modify a table style:

1 Open a table stylesheet.

The TableStyle Editor appears.

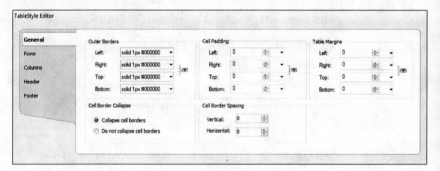

2 On the **General** tab, select the following options:

- ▫ **Outer Borders** — select the style, width, and color of your table borders.

- ▫ **Cell Padding** — select the amount of space between a cell's border and its content.

- ▫ **Table Margins** — select the amount of space between the table and the content around the table.

- ▫ **Cell Border Collapse** — cell borders normally appear inside row borders. If you collapse them, they are merged with the row border.

- ▫ **Cell Border Spacing** — select the amount of space between cells.

3 Select the **Rows** tab.

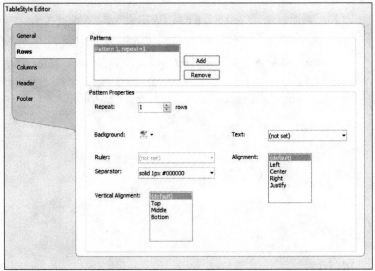

4 On the **Rows** tab, select the following options:

- **Patterns** — patterns can be used to provide different row formats, such as alternating background colors.

- **Pattern Properties** — if you use a pattern, select how many times the pattern should repeat, its background color, text color, and a separator border.

5 Select the **Columns** tab.

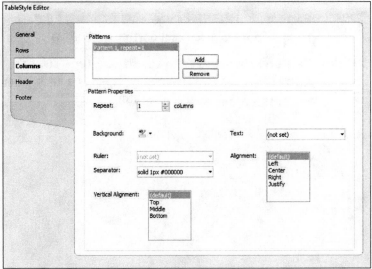

6 On the **Columns** tab, select the following options:

- **Patterns** — patterns can be used to provide different column formats, such as alternating background colors.

- **Pattern Properties** — if you use a pattern, select how many times the pattern should repeat, its background color, text color, and a separator border.

7 Select the **Header** tab.

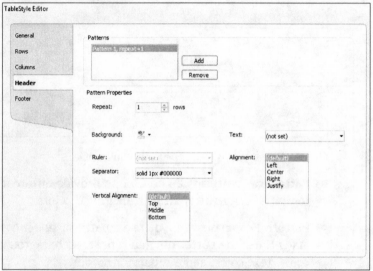

8 On the **Header** tab, select the following options:

- **Patterns** — patterns can be used to provide different header formats, such as a bottom border.

- **Pattern Properties** — if you use a pattern, select how many times the pattern should repeat, its background color, text color, and a separator border.

9 Select the **Footer** tab.

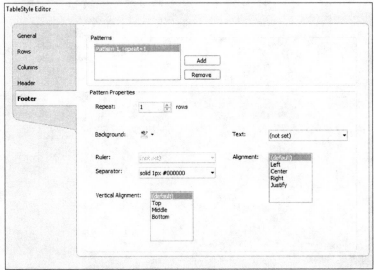

10 On the **Footer** tab, select the following options:

- □ **Patterns** — patterns can be used to provide different footer formats, such as a top border.

- □ **Pattern Properties** — if you use a pattern, select how many times the pattern should repeat, its background color, text color, and a separator border.

To assign a table style to a table:

1 Click inside the table.

2 Select **Table** > **Table Properties**.
The Table Properties dialog box appears.

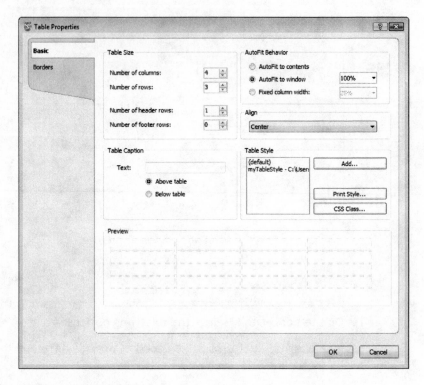

3   Select a **Table Style**.

4   Click **OK**.

Removing inline formatting from a table

If a table contains inline formatting, the inline formatting will override the formatting in your table style. For example, if your table contains inline formatting that adds red borders, the borders will be red even if the table stylesheet specifies black borders.

Inline table formatting is often found in topics that are imported from RoboHelp or Word.

Shortcut	Toolbar	Menu
Alt+A, T, S	none	Table > Table Style > Reset Local Formatting

To remove inline formatting from a table:

1 Click inside the table.

2 Select **Table** > **Table Style** > **Reset Local Formatting**.

Images, videos, and sounds

You can use any of the following image, video, and sound file types:

Image file types

- Bmp
- emf (or wmf)
- **gif**
- hdp (or wdp)
- **jpg** (or jpeg)
- **png**
- tif (or tiff)
- wdp
- xaml
- xps (or exps)

Video file types

- asf (or asx)
- mov
- mp4
- **mpg (or mpeg)**
- **swf**
- qt

Sound file types

- au
- midi (or mid)
- **mp3**
- **wav**
- wma

The most popular formats are in bold.

Inserting an image

You can insert images into topics, snippets, master pages, and page layouts. By default, images are stored in the Resources\Images folder.

✎ You can create a style to display images as small 'thumbnails' that users can enlarge when needed. See 'Creating an image thumbnail style' on page 162.

Shortcut	Toolbar	Menu
Alt+I, P	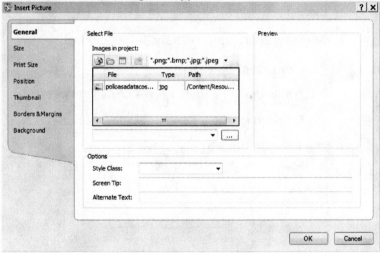 (XML Editor toolbar)	Insert > Picture

To insert an image:

1 Open a file.

2 In the XML Editor, place your cursor where you want to insert the image.

3 Click in the XML Editor toolbar.
   —OR—
   Select **Insert > Picture**.

   The Insert Picture dialog box appears.

4 Select an image in the Images in Project list.
   —OR—
   Click and select an image.

5 Type a **Screen Tip**.
   Screen tips are recommended by accessibility guidelines such as the US Government's Section 508 and the W3C's Web Content Accessibility Guidelines (WCAG).

6 Click **OK**.

Inserting a video NEW!

You can insert Flash (swf), Windows Media Player (asf and mpg), or Quicktime (mov, mp4, and qt) videos into topics, snippets, and master pages. Support for asf, mpg, mov, mp4, and qt files is new in Flare 6.

By default, videos are stored in the Resources\Multimedia folder.

Shortcut	Toolbar	Menu
Alt+I, M	none	Insert > Multimedia

To insert a video:

1 Open a file.

2 In the XML Editor, place your cursor where you want to insert the movie.

3 Select **Insert >Multimedia** and select either:

  □ **Flash** — swf movies

  □ **Windows Media Player** — asf or mpg movies

  □ **Quicktime** —mov, mp4, or qt movies

The Insert Multimedia dialog box appears.

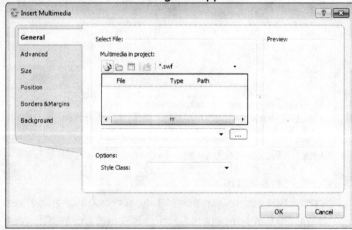

4 Select a movie in the Multimedia in Project list.
—OR—
Click 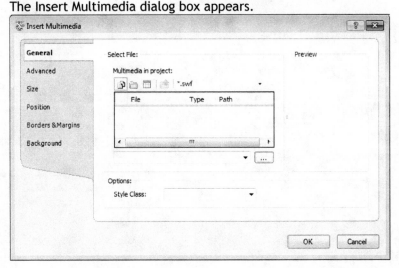 and select a movie.

5 Click **OK**.
The movie appears in your file as a grey box, but it will play normally in the preview and in your targets.

Inserting a sound NEW!

You can insert sounds into topics, snippets, and master pages. By default, sounds are stored in the Resources\Multimedia folder.

Shortcut	Toolbar	Menu
Alt+I, P	(XML Editor toolbar)	Insert > Picture

To insert a sound:

1 Open a file.

2 In the XML Editor, place your cursor where you want to insert the sound.

3 Select **Insert >Multimedia > Windows Media Player**.
The Insert Multimedia dialog box appears.

4 Select a sound in the Multimedia in Project list.

—OR—

Click ⬚ and select a sound.

5 Click **OK**.

The sound appears in your file as a grey box, but it will play normally in the preview and in your targets.

'How do I see which files use an image, video, or sound?'

You can right-click any multimedia file and select **Show Dependencies** to view a list of topics that include it. In fact, you can right-click any file, including stylesheets, topics, and JavaScript files, to see its dependencies.

Sample questions for this section

1 Which of the following statements is true?

A) You can create HTML or XHTML topics with Flare.

B) You must know HTML or XML to use Flare.

C) XHTML is an XML schema and is the successor to HTML.

D) All of the above.

2 How many topics can you have open in Flare?

A) One

B) Two (one in the XML editor and one in the Internal Text Editor)

C) Up to twenty

D) As many as you want

3 You can import and link the following types of Flare files between projects:

A) Topics

B) Stylesheets

C) All of the above

4 How do you import a PDF file?

A) Right-click the Imports folder and create a PDF import file.

B) Save the PDF as HTML and import the HTML file.

C) Select **File** > **Import** > **PDF File**.

D) Select **Project** > **Add PDF File**.

5 Table styles files have the following extension:

A) .htm

B) .tss

C) .css

D) .fltbl

6 You can insert the following types of images into a topic:

A) jpg

B) svg

C) eps

D) ai

7 How can you view a list of topics that include an image?

A) Select **View** > **Image List**.

B) Right-click the image in the Content Explorer and select **Show Dependencies**.

C) Hover your cursor over the image in a topic.

D) Open the Images Analyzer report on the **Project Analysis** tab.

Links

This section covers:

- Hyperlinks
- Popup links
- Cross references
- Drop-down, expanding, and toggler links
- Related topic, keyword, and concept links
- Relationship links

Hyperlinks

You can create hyperlinks that open:

- Topics
- Bookmarks in topics
- Documents such as .doc, .xls, and .pdf files
- Websites
- Email messages

You can add hyperlinks anywhere in a topic. They are often included at the end of a topic to suggest related topics. A link's text should clearly identify what will happen when it is clicked. For example:

Email technical support (well-worded link label)

Click here if you have a question (poorly-worded link label)

Unvisited links are usually blue and underlined, and visited links are usually purple and underlined. You can change their appearance by modifying the "a" (for "anchor") style in your stylesheet.

Creating links

Shortcut	Toolbar	Menu
Ctrl+K	(XML Editor toolbar)	Insert > Hyperlink

📰 *If you Ctrl-click a link in the XML Editor, the linked topic opens as a new tab in the XML Editor.*

To create a link to a topic:

1 Open the topic that will contain the link.

2 Highlight the text that you want to use as the link.
—OR—
Click an image and select **Select**.

3 Click 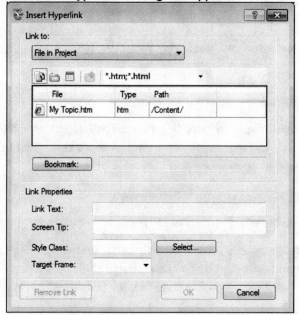 in the XML Editor toolbar.

—OR—

Select **Insert > Hyperlink**.

—OR—

Press **Ctrl+K**.

The Insert Hyperlink dialog box appears.

4 In the **Link to** section, select **File in Project**.

5 Select a topic.

TIP *You can click the 📁 icon to view the topics organized by folder rather than file name.*

6 Type a **Screen Tip**.

Screen tips are recommended by accessibility guidelines such as Section 508 of the U.S Government's Rehabilitation Act and the W3C's Web Content Accessibility Guidelines (WCAG).

7 If needed, select a **Style Class** for the link.

8 Select a **Target Frame**.

The target frame specifies where the link will appear. For example, you can select 'New Window' to open the link in a new window. By default, the link will open in the current window.

9 Click **OK**.
The hyperlink is added to the topic.

To create a link to a document:

1 Locate the document to which you want to link.

2 Copy the document to the Content folder.

3 Open the topic that will contain the link.

4 Highlight the text that you want to use as the link.
—OR—
Click an image and select **Select**.

5 Click in the XML Editor toolbar.
—OR—
Select **Insert** > **Hyperlink**.
—OR—
Press **Ctrl+K**.

The Insert Hyperlink dialog box appears.

6   In the **Link to** section, select **File in Project**.

7   Select a topic.

8   Type a **Screen Tip**.
    Screen tips are recommended by accessibility guidelines such
    as Section 508 of the U.S Government's Rehabilitation Act and
    the W3C's Web Content Accessibility Guidelines (WCAG).

9   If needed, select a **Style Class** for the link.

10 Select a **Target Frame**.
    The target frame specifies where the link will appear. For
    example, you can select 'New Window' to open the link in a
    new window. By default, the link will open in the current
    window.

11 Click **OK**.
    The hyperlink is added to the topic.

To create a link to a website:

1 Open the topic that will contain the link.

2 Highlight the text that you want to use as the link.
—OR—
Click an image and select **Select**.

3 Click 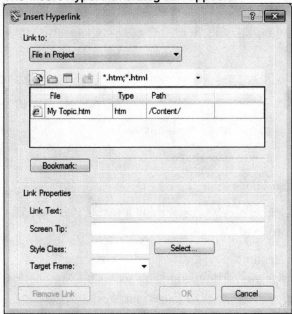 in the XML Editor toolbar.
—OR—
Select **Insert** > **Hyperlink**.
—OR—
Press **Ctrl+K**.
The Insert Hyperlink dialog box appears.

4 In the **Link to** section, select **Website**.

5 Type a website address.

6 Type a **Screen Tip**.
Screen tips are recommended by accessibility guidelines such as Section 508 of the U.S Government's Rehabilitation Act and the W3C's Web Content Accessibility Guidelines (WCAG).

7 If needed, select a **Style Class** for the link.

8 Select a **Target Frame**.
Links to websites often appear in a new window.

9 Click **OK**.
The hyperlink is added to the topic.

Creating image map links

An image map allows you to add links within an image. You can add as many links as needed to an image, and the links can be rectangular, oval, or irregular shapes. For example, you could add links to a picture of the United States so that each state was a link.

To create an image map link:

1 Open the topic that contains the picture to which you want to add links.

2 Click the image and select **Image Map**.
The Image Map Editor window appears.

3 If the image appears faded, click .

4 Select an image map shape.

5 Draw your image map.

6 In the **Link to** section, select a link target type, such as a topic or website, and a target.

7 Type a **Screen Tip**.
Screen tips are recommended by accessibility guidelines such as Section 508 of the U.S Government's Rehabilitation Act and the W3C's Web Content Accessibility Guidelines (WCAG).

8 Select a **Target Frame**.

9 Click **OK**.

10 Click **OK** in the Image Map Editor toolbar.
The Image Map Editor closes, and the image map is added to your image.

'How do I view a topics' links?' NEW!

You can view a list of links by opening a topic (or any type of file) and selecting **View** > **Link Viewer**.

Finding and fixing broken links

You can use the Broken Links analyzer report to find and fix broken links in your project. Broken links are not a common problem, but they can occur when you import content with broken links or if you delete a topic and don't click **Remove Links**.

To find and fix broken links:

1 Select **View** > **Project Analysis**.

2 Select **Broken Links**.
   A list of broken links appears.

3 Double-click a broken link in the list.
   The topic opens in the XML Editor, and the broken link is highlighted.

4 Right-click the highlighted link and select **Edit Hyperlink**.

5 Select a new link location.

6 Click **OK**.

Popup links

You can create two types of popup links: topic popups and text popups.

Topic popups are links that open another topic in a popup window. Since a popup link opens another topic, the popup content can contain formatted text, images, tables, and lists.

Text popups are links that display hidden text in a popup window. They can only contain unformatted text. Since the popup's content is hidden inside the topic that contains the link, you cannot reuse a text popup in multiple topics. Instead, you must retype the content in each topic.

Creating a topic popup link

You can create topic popup links to open topics or other documents in a popup window. They are often used to provide definitions for terms and acronyms.

Like a 'normal' link, a topic popup link opens another topic. The difference is that the topic opens in a popup window that closes when it loses focus. A normal link can open in a new window, but the new window will not automatically close. Flare can automatically size the popup window based on the popup's content, or you can specify the width and height in your stylesheet.

Popup links are also similar to drop-down, expanding, and toggler links. However, drop-down, expanding, and toggler links show and hide content in the current topic rather than in a popup window. Popup links are not as popular as these other link types because they can cause problems with popup blockers and because they can be hard to print. See 'Drop-down, expanding, and toggler links' on page 103.

Shortcut	Toolbar	Menu
Alt+I, T	none	Insert > Topic Popup

To create a topic popup link:

1 Open the topic that will contain the link.

2 Highlight the text that you want to use as the link.
 —OR—
 Click an image and select **Select**.

3 Select **Insert** > **Topic Popup**.
 The Insert Topic Popup dialog box appears.

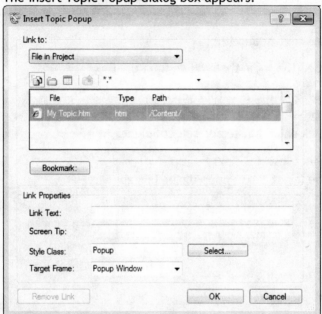

4 In the **Link to** section, select a link target type, such as a topic or website, and select a link target.

5 Type a **Screen Tip**.
 Screen tips are recommended by accessibility guidelines such as Section 508 of the U.S Government's Rehabilitation Act and the W3C's Web Content Accessibility Guidelines (WCAG).

6 Click **OK**.
 The popup link is added to the topic.

Creating a text popup link

Text popups can only display unformatted text. The popup's content is stored inside the topic that contains the link, so you cannot reuse a text-only popup in another topic without retyping the popup's content.

Shortcut	Toolbar	Menu
Alt+I, X	none	Insert > Text Popup

To create a text popup link:

1 Open the topic that will contain the link.

2 Highlight the text that you want to use as the link.
   —OR—
   Click on an image and select **Select**.

3 Select **Insert** > **Text Popup**.
   The Insert Text Popup dialog box appears.

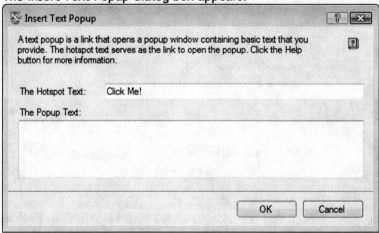

4 Type the popup text.

5 Click **OK**.
   The popup link appears.

Cross references

Cross reference links provide two advantages over 'normal' links:

- ▫ The link's label can use a variable to include the target topic's title
- ▫ The link's label can include page numbers for print targets

If a cross reference's link label uses a variable to include the target topic's title, the label will be automatically updated if you change the topic's title.

Cross reference labels can be set up using a cross reference style named 'MadCap|xref.' You can set up the style to automatically add words, format, or add page numbers to your cross reference labels.

Creating a cross reference

Shortcut	Toolbar	Menu
Ctrl+Shift+R	(XML Editor toolbar)	Insert > Cross Reference

To create a cross reference:

1 Open a topic.

2 Position your cursor where you want to insert the cross reference.

3 Click in the XML Editor toolbar.
—OR—
Select **Insert > Cross Reference**.
—OR—
Press **Ctrl+Shift+R**.

The Insert Cross Reference dialog box appears.

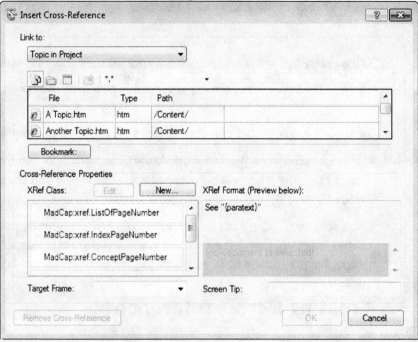

4   For **Link To**, select **Topic in Project**.

5   Select a topic.
    TIP *You can click the* 📁 *icon to view the topics organized by folder rather than file name.*

6   Click **OK**.

Drop-down, expanding, and toggler links

You can create three types of 'show/hide' links: drop-down, expanding, and toggler. By default, these links can include expanded/collapsed arrow icons. You can change or remove these icons by modifying the link styles.

'What's the difference?'

A **drop-down** link shows and hides a paragraph, image, or list item *below* the drop-down link. Drop-down links are often used to show and hide content between subheadings.

An **expanding** link shows and hides a word or sentence *within* a paragraph or list item. Expanding links are often used to show and hide short definitions.

A **toggler** link shows and hides a named element (such as a paragraph, image, or list item) *anywhere* in a topic. Toggler links are often used to show and hide a screenshot or table from a link at the top of a topic.

Creating a drop-down link

Shortcut	Toolbar	Menu
Alt+I, D	none	Insert > Drop-Down Text

To create a drop-down link:

1 Open the topic that will contain the drop-down link.

2 Type and highlight the drop-down link and drop-down text.

3 Select **Insert > Drop-Down Text.**

The Insert Drop-Down dialog box appears.

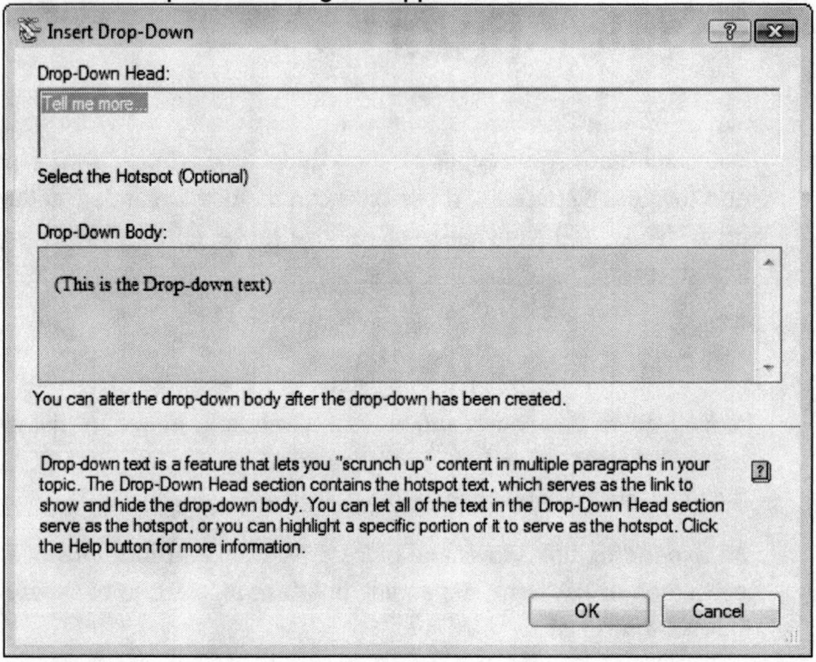

4 Highlight the text you want to use as the drop-down link (or 'head').

5 Click **OK**.

The ⏷ drop-down icon appears to the left of the drop-down link.

Creating an expanding link

Shortcut	Toolbar	Menu
Alt+I, E	none	Insert > Expanding Text

To create an expanding link:

1 Open the topic that will contain the expanding text link.

2 Highlight the expanding link and text.

3 Select **Insert > Expanding Text**.

The Insert Expanding Text dialog box appears.

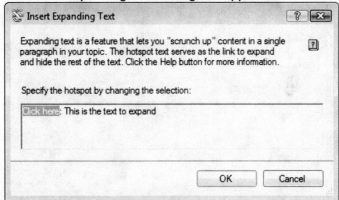

4 Highlight the text that you want to use as the link.

5 Click **OK**.

The |T| expanding text link icon appears after the expanding text link.

Creating a toggler link

Shortcut	Toolbar	Menu
Alt+I, L	none	Insert > Toggler

To create a toggler link:

1 Open the topic that will contain the toggler link.

2 Click inside or highlight the toggler content block.

3 Select **Format > Name**.

4 Type a name for the toggled element.

5 Click **OK**.

6 If needed, assign the same name to other content blocks.

7 In the topic, highlight the text that you want to use as the toggler link.

8 Select **Insert** > **Toggler**.

The Insert Toggler dialog box appears.

9 Select a toggler target by checking its checkbox.

Remember, you can associate more than one toggler target with a toggler link.

10 Click **OK**.

The ⊺ toggler icon appears to the left of the toggler text.

Related topic, keyword, and concept links

You can add related topic, keyword, and concept (also known as "see also") links to your topics. When the user clicks one of these links, a popup window appears with a list of topics:

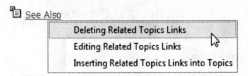

 Related topic, keyword, and concept links are automatically removed when you create a print target.

'What's the difference?'

All three of these links open a popup list of topics. The difference between them is how you select the topics that appear in the list.

Related topics links display a list of topics that you have manually selected. They are easier to create than keyword and concept links, but they are much harder to update. If you need to update a related topics link, you must manually add topics to or remove topics from the list.

Keyword links display a list of topics that include the specified index term(s) (or 'keywords'). If you remove a keyword from or add a keyword to a topic, all of the keyword links that use the keyword are automatically updated.

Concept links display a list of topics that include the same concept term. If you remove a concept term from or add a concept term to a topic, all of the concept links that use that concept term are automatically updated.

Creating a related topics link

Shortcut	Toolbar	Menu
none	none	Insert > Help Control > Related Topics Control

To create a related topic link:

1 Open the topic that will contain the related topics link.

2 Position your cursor where you want to insert the related topics link.

3 Select **Insert > Help Control > Related Topics Control**.
   The Insert Related Topics Control dialog box appears.

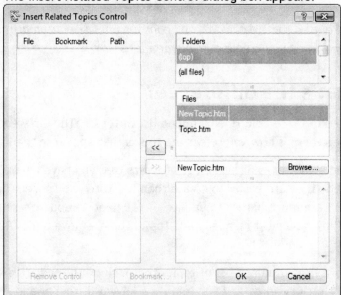

4 Select the **Folder** that contains the topic.

5 Select a topic in the **Files** section.

6 Click to add the topic to the related topics link.

7 Add more topics as needed.

8 Click **OK**.
   The related topics link appears in your topic.

Creating a keyword link

Before you create keyword links, you will need to add index keywords to your topics. When you create a keyword link, you select a keyword to include all of the topics that contain the keyword. See 'Indexes' on page 133 for information about adding keywords to topics.

Shortcut	Toolbar	Menu
none	none	Insert > Help Control > Keyword Link Control

To create a keyword link:

1 Open the topic that will contain the keyword link.

2 Position your cursor where you want to insert the keyword link.

3 Select **Insert** > **Help Control** > **Keyword Link Control**.
The Insert Keyword Link Control dialog box appears.

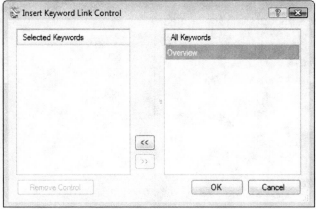

4 Select a keyword.

5 Click <<< to add the keyword to the keyword link.

6 Add more keywords as needed.

7 Click **OK**.
The keyword link appears in your topic.

   Keyword links do not work in the preview.

Creating a concept link

Before you create a concept link, you need to add concept terms to your topics. When you create a concept link, you select a concept term to include all of the topics that contain the concept term.

Shortcut	Toolbar	Menu
none	none	Insert > Help Control > Concept Link

To add a concept term:

1 Open a topic to associate with the concept term.

2 Position the cursor where you want to add the concept term.

3 Select **Tools** > **Concepts** > **Concept Window**.
—OR—
Press **Shift+F9**.

The Concepts window appears.

4 Type a concept term and press **Enter**.

5 Type more terms as needed.

6 Click **Save**.

To add a concept link:

1 Open the topic that will contain the concept link.

2 Position your cursor where you want to insert the concept link.

3 Select **Insert** > **Help Control** > **Concept Link**.
The Insert Concept Link Control dialog box appears.

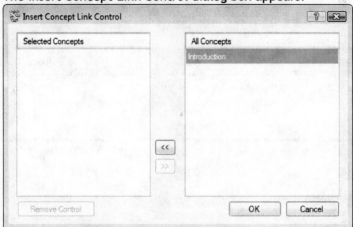

4 Select a concept term.

5 Click <<< to add the concept term to the concept link.

6 Click **OK**.
The concept link is added to the topic.

Concept links do not work in the preview.

Relationship links

You can create relationship tables to organize your topics by type. For example, you can create a relationship table to specify how the following topics are related to each other:

Relationship	Concept	Task	Reference
soccer	defense.htm	goalkeeping.htm	rules.htm
	offense.htm	passing.htm	
		shooting.htm	

This relationship table could be used to add the following links to your topics:

Related Information
  Defense
  Offense

Related Tasks
  Goalkeeping
  Passing
  Shooting

Reference Materials
  Rules

'How are relationship links different from help controls?'

There are four key differences between relationship links and help controls such as related topic, keyword, and concept links:

1 **How they are created and applied**
Relationship links are created based on relationship tables, and you can associate different relationship tables with different targets.

Help controls are created by manually selecting topics or by automatically selecting topics that contain selected keyword or concept markers.

2   **Link grouping**
Relationship tables are used to specify how topics are related based on topic types such as concept, tasks,and reference. Relationship links can separate links based on their type and display link group headings such as 'Related Information,' 'Related Tasks,' and 'Reference Materials.'

Help controls display the links in one list.

3   **Appearance**
Relationship links appear in the topic.

Help control links appear in a popup window.

4   **Print support**
Relationship links will appear in print targets.

Help control links do not appear in print targets.

Creating a relationship table

You can use one relationship table for your project, or you can create multiple relationship tables and use them for different targets.

Shortcut	Toolbar	Menu
Alt-P, V, R	none	Project > Advanced > Add Relationship Table

To create a relationship table:

1   Select **Project** > **Advanced** > **Add Relationship Table**.
The Add Relationship Table dialog box appears.

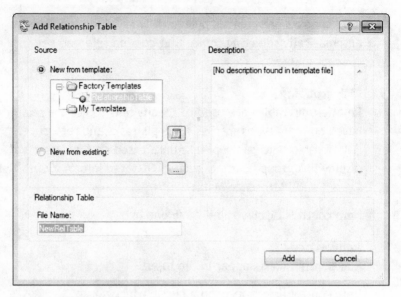

2   Select a **Source** template.

3   Type a **File Name**.

4   Click **Add**.
The Relationship Table Editor appears.

Adding a relationship to a relationship table

Relationships are used to group topics by type. For example, you can create a relationship to group five topics about printing to specify whether each topic is a conceptual, task, or reference topic.

To add a relationship to a relationship table:

1   Open a relationship table.

2   Click ![icon] to create a new row.

3   Click ![icon].
The Row Properties dialog box appears.

4   Type a name for the row.

5   Click **OK**.

6 Click the **Concept**, **Task**, or **Reference** cell.

7 Click 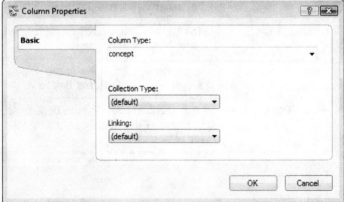.

8 Select a topic and click **OK**.

Adding a column to a relationship table

By default, relationship tables include concept, task, and reference columns. You can add columns to specify other types of topic relationships.

To add a column to a relationship table:

1 Open a relationship table.

2 Click inside a column. The new column will be added to the left of the selected column.

3 Click .

4 Click .
The Column Properties dialog box appears.

5 Type a column name in the Column Type text box.

6 Select a **Collection Type**.

Type	Description
Unordered	Creates an unordered list of links.
Family	Creates links to topics in the row and all of the topics in the same cell.
Sequence	Creates links based on their order in the relationship table. This option is only available for DITA topics.
Choice	Allows you to highlight a link in the group. This option is only available for DITA topics.
Use CONREF target	Uses the CONREF attribute determine the links. This option is only available for DITA topics.

7 Select a **Linking** option.

Option	Description
Source Only	The topic will link to other topics, but other topics will not link back to it.
Target Only	The topic will not link to other topics, but other topics will link to it.
Normal	The topic will link to other topics, and other topics will link to it.
None	The topic will not link to other topics, and other topics will not link to it.
Use CONREF target	Uses the CONREF attribute determine the links. This option is only available for DITA topics.

8 Click **OK**.

Creating a relationship link

You can add relationship links to your topics to automatically insert links into your topics based on the defined relationships in a relationships table.

Shortcut	Toolbar	Menu
Alt-I, Y, A	none	Insert > Proxy > Insert Relationships Proxy

To create a relationship link:

1 Open the topic that will contain the relationship link.

2 Position your cursor where you want to insert the link.

3 Select **Insert > Proxy > Insert Relationships Proxy**.
The Relationships Proxy dialog box appears.

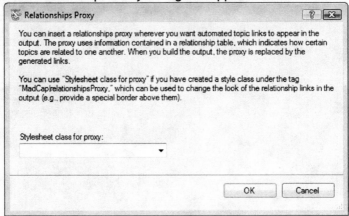

4 Click **OK**.
The relationships proxy appears in your topic.

Associating a relationship table with a target

You can create and use different relationship tables for each target to control which links appear in your topics.

To associate a relationship table with a target:

1 Open a target.

2 Select the **Relationship Table** tab.

3 Select the **Relationship Table(s)** to use.

4 Save the target.

Sample questions for this section

1 How can you view a list of topics that link to a topic?
A) Highlight the topic and select **View** > **Links**.
B) Right-click the topic in the Content Explorer and select **Show Dependencies**.
C) Right-click the topic and select **Topic Properties**.
D) Open the Link Viewer.

2 How can you find and fix broken links?
A) Click each link in the XML Editor.
B) Select **Project** > **Check Links**.
C) Open the Project Analyzer tab and select the **Link** report.
D) Select **Edit** > **Find and Replace** and search for broken links.

3 What is an image map?
A) A list of all of the images in your project.
B) An image that shows how your topics are linked together.
C) A list of links, like a site map, that users can use to open topics.
D) An image that contains links.

4 How do you change the link label for a cross reference?
A) Change the **Link Label** in the Cross References dialog box.
B) Change the MadCap|xref style properties.
C) Right-click the cross reference and select **Edit Link Label**.
D) You can't—it's always set to the link's topic title.

5 Which type of link can open a web page? (select all that apply)
A) Hyperlink
B) Popup
C) Text popup
D) Cross reference

6 Which type of link can show and hide content *below* the link?
A) Expanding links
B) Drop-down links
C) Toggler links
D) Drop-down and toggler links

7 Which type of link does not work in Flare's preview window?
A) Popup links
B) Cross references
C) Expanding links
D) Keyword links

Navigation

This section covers:

- TOCs
- Index
- Search
- Browse sequences
- Glossaries

TOCs

A table of contents ('TOC') is an ordered list of links that your users can use to find and open topics. Most TOCs start with introductory topics and end with troubleshooting and advanced topics.

A TOC contains books and pages. Books are used to organize pages and add levels to your TOC. They can link to topics, or they can simply be used to group pages. Pages always link to topics or other content. A page does not have to be inside a book. For example, a 'What's New' page is often placed at the beginning of a TOC to draw the user's attention.

You don't have to include every topic in your TOC. If you don't include a topic in your TOC, it won't be included when you create a print target.

TOC books and pages usually link to topics, but they can also link to websites, email addresses, other TOCs, browse sequences, and documents such as .doc, .xls, and .pdf files.

TOCs are stored in an XML-based .fltoc file in the Project Organizer.

Moving the TOC to the accordion TIP▷

You can move the TOC Editor to the accordion if you want to use your TOC as an alternative to the Content Explorer. You can even Ctrl-click a book or page in the TOC to open its associated topic in the XML Editor.

Shortcut	Toolbar	Menu
Ctrl+Shift+D	none	Window > Send to Other Dock

To dock the TOC Editor:

1 Open your TOC in the TOC Editor.

2 Select **Window** > **Send to Other Dock**.
   Your TOC will move to the left dock.

Creating a TOC

When you create a project, Flare creates a blank TOC for you. You can use this TOC, or you can create your own.

'Can I create multiple TOCs?'

Yes, you can create multiple TOCs in a project. If you create multiple TOCs, you can use different TOCs for different targets. For example, you can include different topics and organize your topics in a different order for a print and online targets. You can also create multiple TOCs if you have multiple authors. You can link each author's TOC together into a master TOC.

Shortcut	Toolbar	Menu
Alt+P, L	none	Project > Add Table of Contents

To create a TOC:

1 Select **Project** > **Add Table of Contents**.
   —OR—
   Right-click the TOCs folder and select **Add Table of Contents**.
   The Add TOC dialog box appears.

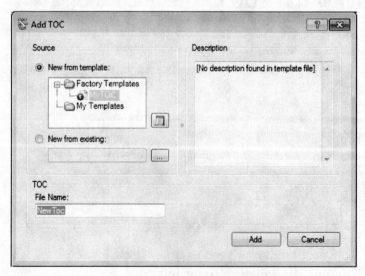

2 Select a **Source** template.

3 Type a **File Name**.

4 Click **Add**.
The TOC appears in the TOC folder in the Project Organizer and opens in the TOC Editor.

Creating TOC books and pages

Flare provides multiple ways to create TOC books and pages. You can click the new TOC book or new page icons, type a title, and select a link. Or, you can drag a topic from the Content Explorer to the TOC. You can even drag a folder to the TOC and auto-create a book for the folder and pages for each topic inside the book.

To create a TOC book:

1 Open a TOC.

2 Click ▢ in the TOC Editor toolbar.
A new TOC book named **New TOC Book** appears.

3 Type a name for the book.

4 If necessary, move the book to a new location in the TOC.
You can drag-and-drop the TOC book or use the arrows in the TOC Editor toolbar.

To create a TOC page:

1 Open a TOC.

2 If you want to add a page inside a book, select the book.

3 Click ▢ in the TOC Editor toolbar.
A new TOC page named 'New Entry' appears.

4 Double-click the TOC page.
—OR—
Click ▣ in the TOC Editor toolbar.

The Properties dialog box appears.

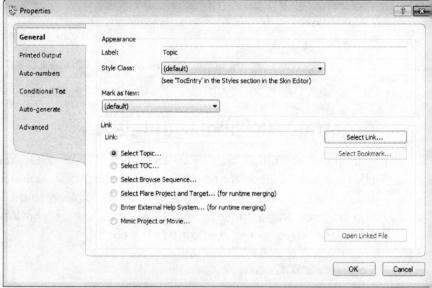

5 Type a **Label** for the page.

6 Click **Select link**.
   The Link to Topic dialog box appears.

7 Select a topic.

8 Click **Open**.

9 Click **OK**.

A flag ( ) icon appears beside TOC books and pages that are not linked. A broken link ( ) icon appears beside books and pages that have broken links.

Finding and fixing issues in a TOC NEW!

In Flare 6, you can find and fix TOC books and pages that are not linked or have broken links.

To find and fix TOC issues:

1 Open a TOC.

2 If your TOC books are intentionally unlinked, click .

3 Click .

   The first issue is highlighted. Unlinked items are marked with a icon. Broken links are marked with a icon.

4 Right-click the TOC item and select **Properties**.
   The Properties dialog box appears.

5 On the **General** tab, select a new link and click **OK**.

Auto-generating TOC books and pages

If you have a long topic with multiple subheadings, you can auto-generate TOC pages to link to the subheadings. For example, the following topic has one main heading and four sub-headings:

> **South Africa** (formatted as Heading 1)
> *Cape Town* (Heading 2)
> *Durban* (Heading 2)
> *Johannesburg* (Heading 2)
> *Pretoria* (Heading 2)

You can auto-create the following TOC entries for this topic:

South Africa

   Cape Town
   Durban
   Johannesburg
   Pretoria

To auto-generate TOC entries:

1 Double-click a TOC page.
   The Properties dialog box appears.

2 Select the **Auto-generate** tab.

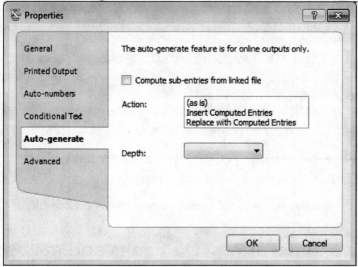

3 Select **Compute sub-entries from linked file**.

4 Select an **Action**.

- □ **Insert Computed Entries** adds the TOC entries below the selected TOC entry.

- □ **Replace with Computed Entries** replaces the selected TOC entry with the new entries.

5 Select a heading **Depth**.
The heading depth is the level of subheadings that should be automatically included in the TOC. For example, selecting **2** will include pages for all heading levels 1 and 2.

6 Click **OK**.

Linking TOCs

If you create multiple TOCs, you can create a link from one TOC to another TOC.

To link TOCs:

1 Open a TOC.

2 Select the location in the TOC where you want to add the link to the other TOC.

3 Click 🖹.
A new TOC entry named 'New entry' appears.

4 Select the new entry and click 🖹.
The Properties dialog box appears.

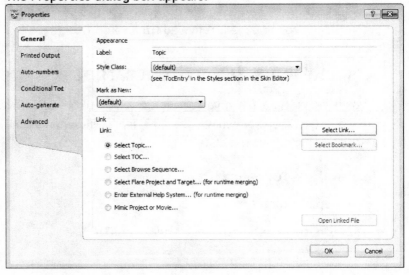

5 Click **Select TOC**.
The Link to TOC dialog box appears.

6 Select the TOC to which you want to link the page.

7 Click **Open**.

8 Click **OK**.

The icon in the TOC Editor changes to 🔘, indicating that the page is linked to a TOC.

Deleting a TOC book or page

You can delete books or pages from your TOC. If you delete a book or page, Flare does not delete the topic to which it is linked.

To delete a TOC book or page:

1 Open a TOC.

2 Select a book or page.

3 Press **Delete**.
—OR—
Click ✕.

The book or page is removed from your TOC.

Associating a TOC with a target

If you have multiple TOCs, you can select a TOC to be used when you build a target. If you only have one TOC, Flare will automatically associate it with your targets.

To associate a TOC with a target:

1 Open a target.

2 On the **General** tab, select a **Master TOC**.

Specifying chapter breaks

If you add chapter breaks to your TOC, you can create separate Word or FrameMaker documents for each chapter.

To specify a chapter break:

1   Open your TOC.

2   Right-click a TOC book or page and select **Properties**. The Properties dialog box appears.

3   Select the **Printed Output** tab.

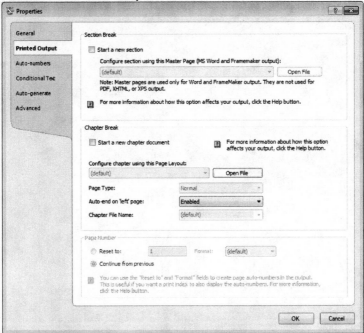

4   Select **Start a new chapter document**.

5   Click **OK**.

Finding topics that are not in the TOC

You can use Flare's Analyzer reports to find topics that are not in a TOC. You don't have to include a topic in a TOC, but this report can help you find topics you may have forgotten to include.

To find topics that are not in a TOC:

1 Select **View** > **Project Analysis**.

2 Select **Topics Not In Selected TOC**.

3 For **Filter**, select a TOC.

▥▷ *You can double-click a topic in the list to open it in the XML Editor.*

Indexes

Like FrameMaker, Flare adds your keywords as markers inside your topics. You can copy a keyword to other topics or delete a keyword when you delete its associated content.

There are four ways to add index entries to topics:

- 'Quick term' method
- Index Window method
- Index Entry Mode method
- Auto-index phrase set method

'Why should I create an index?'

Most users will search your help system instead of using the index. An index also takes much more time to create than the search, since you must add index keywords to your topics. However, a good index is more useful that the search because it only lists the most relevant topics. Another key advantage of the index over the search is that the index is included in print targets.

Adding index entries using the 'quick term' method

The quick term method can be used to quickly add a term to the index while you are writing. Because it's so efficient, I usually use the quick term method to add index terms.

Shortcut	Toolbar	Menu
F10	none	Tools > Index > Insert <term> as Index Keyword

To add a term using the quick term method:

1 Open a topic.

2 Click before the word (or highlight the phrase) that you want to insert as an index term.

3 Select **Tools > Index > Insert <term> as Index Keyword.**
  —OR—
  Press **F10.**

The term is added to the index. If you have Show Markers turned on, the term will appear in a green box.

TIP *To show markers, click* ❬❭ *in the XML Editor toolbar and select* **Show Markers.** *If you can't see the entire index entry, increase the marker width.*

Adding index entries using the Index window method

The Index window can be used to add single word, multiple word, and second-level index entries. The Index window shows all of the index terms within the current topic.

Shortcut	Toolbar	Menu
F9	none	Tools > Index > Index Window

To add an index entry using the Index window:

1 Open a topic.

2 Click before or on the word or phrase that you want to insert as an index term.

3 Select **Tools > Index > Index Window.**
  —OR—
  Press **F9.**
  The Index window appears.

4 Type a term or phrase and press **Enter**.
   The term or phrase is added to the index.

   ▥ *To add a second-level entry, include a colon between the first- and second-level entries.*

Adding index entries using the Index Entry mode method

Index Entry mode is useful when you need to add multiple index entries. When you switch to Index Entry mode, the words you type become index entries rather than topic content. It's a great tool for indexers, since they can focus on indexing and not worry about accidentally changing the content in a topic.

To add an index entry using Index Entry mode:

1 Open a topic.

2 Click ▥ ▾ in the XML Editor toolbar.

3 Position the cursor where you want to add the index term.

4 Type the term and press **Enter**.
   The Index Entry window appears, and the term is added to the index.

5 Continue typing terms as needed. When you are done, click ▥ ▾ in the XML Editor.

Automatically adding index entries

Instead of adding keywords to topics, you can create an auto-index phrase set to automatically add keywords to your topics when you build a target. This method may cause your targets to build more slowly, but you can share the list of keywords across projects.

◇ *If you plan to link your content to a Word or FrameMaker document, you should use this approach because the keywords are added when you generate a target. If you add keywords using the*

*other methods, they will be removed when you re-import the
document.*

To create an auto-index phrase set:

1 Select **Project** > **Advanced** > **Add Auto-index Phrase Set**.
   The Add Auto-index Phrase Set dialog box appears.

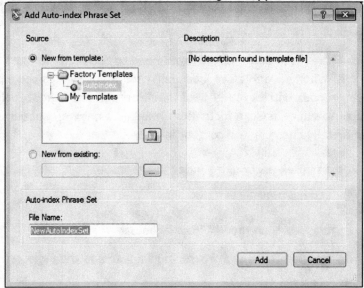

2 Select a **Source** template.

3 Type a **File Name**.

4 Click **Add**.
   The Auto-index Phrase Set is added to the Advanced folder in
   the Project Organizer and appears in the Auto-index Editor.

To add a term to an auto-index phrase set:

1 Open an auto-index phrase set.

2 Click .

The Properties dialog box appears.

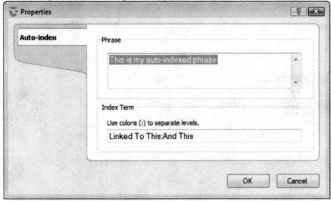

3   Type a **Phrase** to find in your topics.
    The phrase can be the term or something more specific to limit
    the number of index markers Flare adds.

4   Type the **Index Term**.

5   Click **OK**.

*The phrase and index term are case specific. If you want to
add a keyword every time the word 'pizza' or 'Pizza' is used in
your topics, you will need to add two auto-index entries.*

Showing or hiding index entries in a topic

Index entry markers can be distracting when you are not indexing a
topic. You can hide the index markers using the Show Tags icon in the
XML Editor's toolbar.

To show or hide index markers:

1   Click the down arrow beside the ⟨t⟩ ▾ icon.

2   Select **Show Markers**.
    The index markers disappear.

TIP *You can change the size of the markers by modifying the
Marker Width setting.*

Finding topics that are not in the index

You can use Flare's Analyzer reports to find topics that are not in the index.

To find topics that are not in the index:

1 Select **View** > **Project Analysis**.

2 Select **Topics Not In Index**.

▥▷ *You can double-click a topic in the list to open it in the XML Editor.*

Viewing the index

Select **View** > **Index Explorer** to view the index. It displays all of the index entries and their associated topics.

Search

It's very easy to add search to a help system: you only need to select one checkbox!

Most users use the search rather than the TOC or index to find information. When a user searches for a word or phrase, the help system displays a list of all of the topics (by topic titles) that contain the search term(s). When the user opens a topic from the search, the search term is highlighted to make it easy to find.

Adding search synonyms

You can add search synonyms to include terms that do not appear in your topics. You can add two types of synonyms: directional and group.

Directional synonyms are used to associate specific terms with general terms. For example, a directional synonym might associate 'country' with 'New Zealand.' If a user searches for 'country,' the search results would include topics that contain 'country' or 'New Zealand.' However, if the user searches for 'New Zealand,' the results would only include topics that contain 'New Zealand.'

Group synonyms are used to associate a group of equivalent words. For example, a group synonym might include 'close,' 'exit,' and 'quit.' If a user searches for any of these terms, the results would include topics that contain any of these words.

Shortcut	Toolbar	Menu
Alt+P, V, S	none	Project > Advanced > Add Synonym File

To add search synonyms:

1 Select **Project** > **Advanced** > **Add Synonym File**.
The Add Synonyms File dialog box appears.

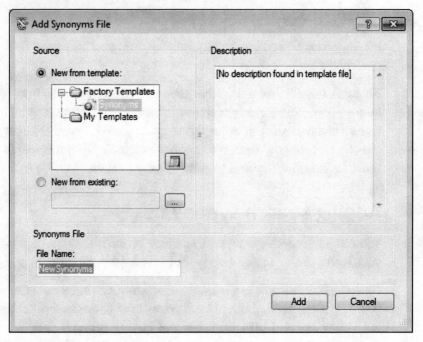

2 Select a **Template Folder** and **Template**.

3 Type a **File Name**.

4 Click **Add**.
The synonym file is added to the Advanced folder in the Project
Organizer and appears in the Synonym Editor.

To add a directional synonym:

1 Open a synonym file.

2 Select the **Directional** tab.

3 Click inside the **Word** cell beside the asterisk (*) and type the
general term.

4 Click inside the **Synonym** cell and type the specific term.

5 If you want to also search for past tense and plural forms of the terms, select the **Stem** option.

To add a group synonym:

1 Open a synonym file.

2 Select the **Groups** tab.

3 Click inside the **Group** cell beside the asterisk (*) and type the terms separated by the = sign.
For example, **close=exit=quit**.

4 Click inside the **Synonym** cell and type the specific term.

5 If you want to also search for past tense and plural forms of the terms, select the **Stem** option.

Excluding a topic in the full-text search

You can hide a topic in the full-text search for WebHelp and DotNet Help. Many help authors use this feature to hide field-level help topics in the search.

To exclude a topic in the full-text search:

1 Right-click a topic in the Content Explorer or File List and select **Properties**.
—OR—
Select a topic and press **F4**.

2 Select the **Topic Properties** tab.

3 Deselect the **Include topic when full-text search database is generated** option.

4 Click **OK**.

Glossaries

Flare provides two glossary features: a combined glossary tab/page that lists all of the terms and definitions, and glossary links that open definitions from your topics.

Glossary terms are stored in a glossary file with a .flglo extension. Glossary files are stored in the Glossaries subfolder in the Project folder.

Creating a glossary

You can use multiple glossaries in a project. For example, you can maintain a glossary of common terms that is shared across multiple projects and another glossary of project-specific terms.

Shortcut	Toolbar	Menu
Alt+P, G	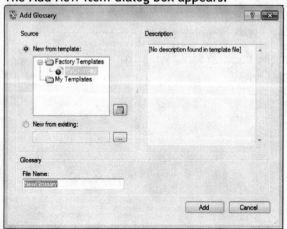	Project > Add Glossary

To create a glossary:

1 Select **Project** > **Add Glossary**.
The Add New Item dialog box appears.

2 Select a **Source** template.

3 Type a **File Name**.
Glossaries have a .flglo extension. If you don't type the extension, Flare will add it for you.

4 Click **Add**.
The glossary appears in the Glossaries folder in the Project Organizer and opens in the Glossary Editor.

Adding glossary terms

You can add terms and definitions directly to a glossary or as you write topics. If you need to include formatting or an image in a definition, you can link to a topic for the definition.

1 Open a glossary.
Glossaries are stored in the Glossaries folder in the Project Organizer.

2 Click ![icon] in the Glossary Editor toolbar.
The Properties dialog box appears.

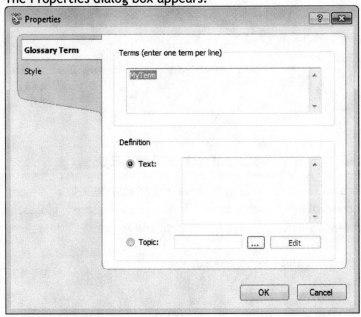

3 Type a glossary **Term**.

4 Type a **Definition** or select a topic that contains the definition.

5 Select the **Style** tab.

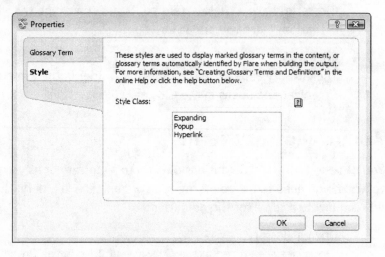

6 Select a style for the glossary link:

- □ **Expanding** — opens the definition with an expanding link

- □ **Popup** — opens the definition in a popup window

- □ **Hyperlink** — closes the current topic and opens the glossary page

  If you don't select a style, Flare will use the 'Popup' style.

7 Click **OK**.

Adding a glossary to a target

To use a glossary in a target, you need to enable it in a skin and associate the skin with a target. You can use different glossaries in different targets, or you can use multiple glossaries in the same target.

To enable a glossary in a skin:

1 Open a skin.

2 On the **General** tab, select the **Glossary** option.

To associate a glossary with a target:

1 Open a target.

2 Select the **Glossary** tab.

3 If you want to include glossary links in your topics, select a **Glossary Term Conversion** method.

4 Select a **Glossary File**.

5 Click **Save**.

'Where's the HTML Help glossary tab?'

HTML Help does not include a glossary tab, and MadCap cannot add one without requiring a .dll file. So, your glossary appears at the bottom of the TOC and opens on the right in the topic pane.

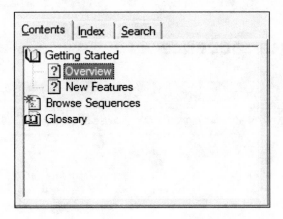

Browse sequences

Like a TOC, a browse sequence is an ordered list of links that can be used to find and open topics. It even uses books and pages like a TOC.

You can create a browse sequence if you want to provide an alternate TOC for your users. For example, you could organize your TOC for technical support users and your browse sequence for managers. Or, you could organize your TOC by complexity (introductory topics first and troubleshooting topics last) and your browse sequence alphabetically.

Browse sequences are stored in a browse sequence file with a .flbrs extension. Browse sequence files are stored in the Advanced subfolder in the Project folder.

Creating a browse sequence

Shortcut	Toolbar	Menu
Alt+P, V, A	none	Project > Advanced > Add Browse Sequence

To create a browse sequence:

1 Select **Project** > **Advanced** > **Add Browse Sequence**.
The Add New Item dialog box appears.

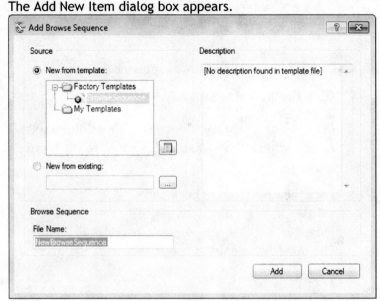

2 Select a **Source** template.

3 Type a **File Name** for the browse sequence.
Browse sequences have a .flbrs extension. If you don't type the extension, Flare will add it for you.

4 Click **Add** and click **OK**.
The browse sequence appears in the Advanced folder in the Project Organizer and opens in the Browse Sequence Editor.

To add books to a browse sequence:

1 Open the browse sequence.

2 Open the Content Explorer.

3 Drag a folder from the Content Explorer to the browse sequence.

4 If you need to rename the browse sequence book:

    □ Click the selected new book entry.
    —OR—

Press **F2**.

The text for the entry is highlighted.

   □   Type the new name.

To manually add books to a browse sequence:

1   Open the browse sequence.

2   Click or ☝ in the Browse Sequence Editor toolbar.
A book named 'New TOC Book' is added to the browse sequence.

3   Click the selected new book entry.
   —OR—
   Press **F2**.
The text for the entry is now highlighted.

4   Type a name for the book.

To add pages to a browse sequence using drag-and-drop:

1   Open the browse sequence.

2   Open the Content Explorer.

3   Drag a topic from the Content Explorer to the browse sequence.

4   If necessary, use the arrows in the browse sequence toolbar to move the page up, down, left or right.

   ⇦ ⇨ ⇧ ⇩

To add pages to a browse sequence using the Browse Sequence Editor:

1   Open the browse sequence.

2   Select the location in the browse sequence where you want to add the new entry.

3 Click in the Browse Sequence Editor.

An entry named 'New entry' is added to the browse sequence.

4 Click the selected new entry.

—OR—

Press **F2**.

The text for the entry is now highlighted.

5 Type a name for the entry and press **Enter**.

6 If necessary, use the arrow buttons in the browse sequence toolbar to move the page left, right, up, or down.

7 Double-click the new entry.

The Properties dialog box appears.

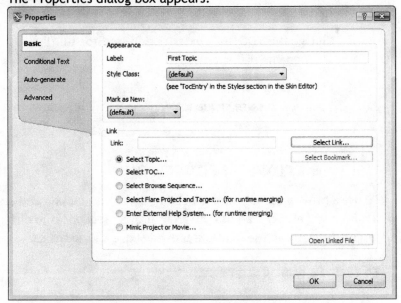

8 If needed, select the **Mark as New** option.

The page will be marked with the 'New' icon: . You can change this icon in your skin.

9 Select **Select Topic**.

10 Click **Select Link**.

The Link to Topic dialog box appears.

11 Select a topic and click **Open**.

12 Click **OK**.

Creating a browse sequence based on your TOC ⏩

Since Flare uses XML for the TOC and browse sequence files, you can make a copy of your TOC and convert it to a browse sequence.

To create a browse sequence based on your TOC:

1 In Windows Explorer, create a copy of your TOC file.
By default, TOC files are located in the Project\TOCs folder.

2 Paste the copy of your TOC file into the Project\Advanced folder.

3 Change the TOC file's extension from .fltoc to .flbrs.
The Rename dialog box appears.

4 Click **Yes**.
Your new browse sequence appears in the Advanced folder in the Project Organizer.

Using a browse sequence

To use a browse sequence, you need to enable it in a skin and associate it with a target. You can use different browse sequences in different targets, or you can use multiple browse sequences in the same target.

To enable a browse sequence in a skin:

1 Open a skin.

2 On the **General** tab, select the **Browse Sequence** option.

3 If you want to include 'next' and 'previous' browse sequence buttons in the WebHelp toolbar:

- □ Select the Topic Toolbar tab.

- □ Select **Enable Custom Layout**.

❑ Add the NextTopic, PreviousTopic, and/or CurrentTopicIndex items to your toolbar.

The three items appear as follows (previous, current, and next):

To associate a browse sequence with a target:

1 Open a target.

2 On the **General** tab, make sure the browse sequence is enabled in the selected skin.

3 Select a **Browse Sequence**.

'Where are my HTML Help browse sequences?'

HTML Help does not include a separate browse sequence feature. Some tools, such as RoboHelp, use a .dll file to add browse sequences to HTML Help. MadCap does not want to require a .dll file for HTML Help, so Flare adds your browse sequence to the bottom of your TOC.

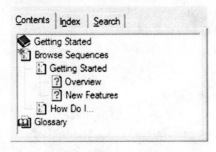

Sample questions for this section

1 Where are your TOC files stored?
A) In the Content Explorer's TOCs folder
B) In the Content Explorer's Resources\TOCs folder
C) In the Project Organizer's TOCs folder
D) In the TOC Explorer

2 Which statement about a TOC is NOT true?
A) Pages must be inside books.
B) Pages can link to topics, Word documents, and web sites.
C) Books can link to topics.
D) Books can contain books.

3 Which character is used to separate first- and second-level index entries?
A) |
B) /
C) :
D) ;

4 How can you view a list of your index terms?
A) Double-click your index in the Project Organizer.
B) Double-click your index in the Content Explorer.
C) Open the Analyzer index report.
D) Select **View** > **Index Explorer**.

5 How do you exclude a topic in the search?
A) Add the topic to your search file in the Project Organizer.
B) Open the Topic Properties dialog box and deselect the **Include topic when full-text search database is generated** option.
C) Do not include the topic in your TOC.
D) You cannot exclude a topic from the search.

6 Where does the glossary appear in HTML Help?
A) As a Glossary accordion item
B) As a Glossary tab
C) At the bottom of the table of contents
D) The glossary does not appear in HTML Help

7 What is a browse sequence?

A) The path the user used to open the topic.

B) An ordered list of links that can be used to find and open topics, like a TOC.

C) A list of related topics at the bottom of topics.

D) A path at the top of your topics that shows how to find this topic in the TOC.

Formatting and design

This section covers:

- Stylesheets
- Master pages
- Page layouts
- Skins

Stylesheets

Like Word templates and FrameMaker catalogs, stylesheets are used to format content. You can define the formatting for each style in a stylesheet, and you can add your own styles (called 'classes') to a stylesheet. You can even specify print- and online-specific styles within a stylesheet to use different formatting for print and online targets.

Stylesheets are stored in the Content Explorer. By default, stylesheets created in Flare are stored in the Resources\Stylesheets folder. If needed, you can move a stylesheet to a different folder.

External and inline styles

Styles that are defined in your cascading stylesheet are called 'external' styles because the formatting is stored in another file rather than in your topics.

You can also format your content directly by highlighting content and changing its appearance. For example, you can highlight a word and make it bold and red. This type of formatting is called 'inline' formatting because the formatting information is stored directly in the topic.

You should avoid using inline formatting. It is much harder to change inline formatting than it is to change a style. If you change a style, all of the topics that use the style are automatically updated when you save the stylesheet. If you need to change inline formatting, you have to change it by hand. Another problem is that inline formatting overrides your styles. It is hard to maintain consistent formatting if you have scattered inline formatting throughout your topics.

If you have inline formatting, you can convert it to a style. See 'Converting inline formatting to a style class' on page 161 for more information.

Creating a stylesheet

Although most Flare projects use the same stylesheet for all topics, you can create multiple stylesheets and apply them to different topics. For example, you could create a 'New Feature' stylesheet so that new topics in your project stand out to your users.

Shortcut	Toolbar	Menu
Alt+P, T	none	Project > Add Stylesheet

To create a stylesheet:

1   Select **Project** > **Add Stylesheet**.
    The Add New Stylesheet dialog box appears.

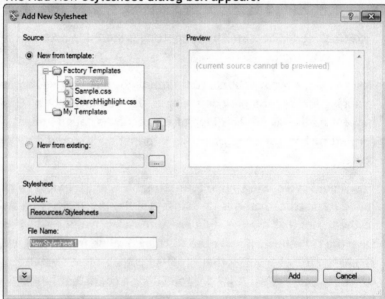

2   Select a **Source** template.

3   Type a **File Name** for the stylesheet.
    Stylesheets have a .css extension. If you don't type the extension, Flare will add it for you.

4   Click **Add**.
    The Copy to Project dialog box appears.

5 Click **OK**.

The stylesheet appears in the Content Explorer and opens in the Stylesheet Editor.

Creating a new style class

You can create your own style classes to format notes, warnings, or other specific types of content. Most style classes are based on the p (paragraph) tag, but you can also create classes for headings, lists, and tables.

To create a style class:

1 Open the stylesheet.

The Stylesheet Editor appears.

2 Select a style.

For example, to create a paragraph class, select **p**.

3 Click **Add Class**.

4 Type a name for the style class.

5 Click **OK**.

Creating an auto-numbering style

You can create an auto-numbering style to automatically number content, including headings, captions, and figures. Auto-numbering styles are often used in print documents.

To create an auto-numbering style:

1 Open the stylesheet.

The Stylesheet Editor appears.

2 Select a style.

For example, to create a paragraph class, select **p**.

3 Click **Add Class**.

4 Type a name for the style class.

5 Click **OK**.

6 Select the new style class.

7 If you are using the Simplified View:

    ▫ Double-click the style class.

    ▫ Select the **Auto-number** tab.

If you are using the Advanced View:

    ▫ In the Show group, select **Property Groups**.

    ▫ Open the **AutoNumber** property group.

    ▫ Select the (not set) value for the **mc-auto-number** property.

8 Type or select an auto-numbering format.

Example	Auto-number Format
1.0 (sample text) 2.0 (sample text)	A:{n+}.{ =0}

I.
    1.1
    1.2
    1.3
	A:{n}.{n+}

I. II. III.	O:{R+}.

I.
    A.
    B.
    C.
	O:{ }{A+}.

Chapter 1	CH:Chapter {chapnum}
Figure 1-1	CF: Figure {chapnum}-{n+}

9 Click **OK**.

10 Click **Save**.

Creating a redacted content style

You can create a redacted content style to 'black out' sensitive, confidential, or private content in a PDF or XPS target. When you apply a redacted style to text, images, or other content, it is permanently replaced with a black rectangle. Users cannot view the original content.

TIP *You can also use a redacted content style to highlight content (rather than black it out) in a PDF or XPS target.*

To create a redacted content style:

1 Open the stylesheet.
The Stylesheet Editor appears.

2 Select a style.
For example, to create a paragraph class, select **p**.

3 Click **Add Class**.

4 Type a name for the style class.

5 Click **OK**.

6 Select the new style class.

7 If you are using the Simplified View:

   □ Double-click the style class.

   □ Select the **Advanced** tab.

   If you are using the Advanced View:

   □ In the Show group, select **Property Groups**.

   □ Open the **Redaction** property group.

   □ Select the (not set) value for the **mc-redacted** property.

8 Select **Redacted**.

9 Click **Save**.

To select how redacted content appears in a PDF or XPS target:

1 Open the target.
The Target Editor appears.

2 Select the **Print Output** tab.

3 Select a **Redacted Text** option: blackout, highlighted, or normal.

Creating an image thumbnail style

You can create a thumbnail style to display smaller 'thumbnail' versions of your images in your targets, and you can specify whether the image displays as full size when the user clicks or moves their mouse over an image.

✎ *You can select* **View** > **Show** > **Show All Images As Thumbnails** *to view all images as thumbnails in the XML Editor.*

To create an image thumbnail style:

1 Open the stylesheet.
The Stylesheet Editor appears.

2 If you are using the Simplified View, click **Advanced View**.

3 Select a style.
For example, to create a paragraph class, select **p**.

4 Click **Add Class**.

5 Type a name for the style class.

6 Click **OK**.

7 Select the new style class.

8 In the Show group, select **Property Groups**.

9 Open the **Thumbnail** property group.

10 Select the (not set) value for the **mc-thumbnail** property.

11 Select how you want the full-size image to appear:

- **hover** - the image appears in a popup window when the user hovers the mouse over the thumbnail

- **link** - the image appears in a new window when the user clicks the thumbnail

- **popup** - the image appears in a popup window when the user clicks the thumbnail

12 Select the (not set) vlaue for the **mc-thumbnail-max-height** or **mc-thumbnail-max-width** property.
Flare will proportionately scale the image, so you don't need to set both properties.

13 Type a maximum width or height.
The default setting is a height of 48px.

14 Click **Save.**

Converting inline formatting to a style class

You can create a style class based on inline formatting. This approach is useful for removing inline formatting or if you prefer to see your formatting as you design it. You can create a style class in the Stylesheet Editor, but sometimes it's easier to create a style by seeing how it will look in your topics.

To create a style based on inline formatting:

1 Open a topic in which you want to use the new style.

2 Use the **Format** menu commands to format the text.

3 Click inside the formatted content.
Do not highlight the content.

4 Select **View > Style Window.**
—OR—
Press **F12.**
The Style window appears.

5 Click **Create Style**.

The Create Style dialog box appears.

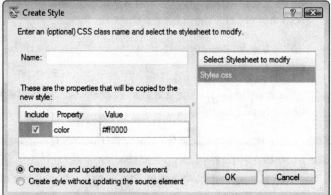

6 In the **Name** field, type a name for the new style without using spaces.

7 If you do not want to include a style property in the new style, deselect its **Include** option.

8 If you want the new style to be applied to the selected content, select **Create style and update the source element**.

If you do not want the new style to be applied to the selected content, select **Create style without updating the source element**.

9 Click **OK**.

The new style is added to the stylesheet.

Modifying a style

You can use Flare's Stylesheet Editor to completely customize your styles.

To modify a style:

1 Open a stylesheet.

The Stylesheet Editor appears.

2 Select the style you want to edit.

If you are using the Advanced view, the selected style's

properties appear on the right. If you are using the Simplified view, double-click the style.

3 Select a property.

4 Select a value to change.

5 Type or select a new value.

6 Modify other properties as needed.

Creating a font set

You can create a font set to specify a list of fonts for a style to use rather than one font family. If you specify a font that is not installed on the user's computer, their browser will use a default font (usually Times). With a font set, you can provide a list of fonts to try before the default font is used.

If you are developing HTML Help or DotNet Help, you should create a font set if you want to use fonts that are not common in Windows. If you are developing WebHelp, you should also create a font set if your users have Mac or Linux computers. Fonts that are commonly installed in Windows might not be available in other operating systems.

To create a font set:

1 Open any topic.

2 Select **Format** > **Font**.
The Font Properties dialog box appears.

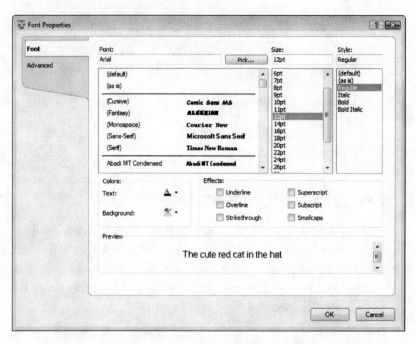

3 Click **Pick**.

The Font Picker dialog box appears.

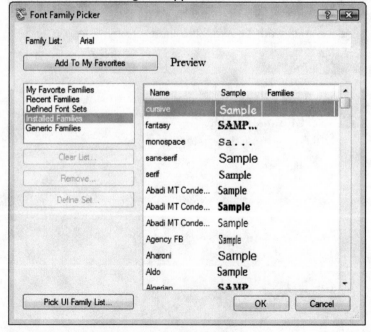

4 Select **Defined Font Sets**.

5 Click **Define Set.**

6 Type a **Name** for the font set.

7 In order, select the fonts you want to include and add them to the list.

8 Click **OK** three times.

You can now use your font set when you select a font for your styles.

Using the print style medium

Flare's built-in 'print' medium is often used when creating print targets. For example, you can set up the print medium to use a different font than online targets.

I often use the print medium to set automatic page breaks for heading 1s and to format my TOC and index styles.

To set automatic page breaks before headings:

1 Open your stylesheet.
Stylesheets are stored in the Resources folder in the Content Explorer.

2 Click **Advanced View.**

3 Select the **Print** medium.

4 Select a heading style, such as **h1.**

5 Open the **PrintSupport** property group.

6 Change the **page-break-before** option.
You can set the option to always add a page break or to start the heading on the left or right.

To format the TOC and index styles:

1 Open your stylesheet.
Stylesheets are stored in the Resources folder in the Content Explorer.

2 Select the **Print** medium.

3 Click the plus sign beside the **p** style.

4 Select a TOC or index class.

5 Modify the style's properties. For example, to remove the dotted line from a TOC style, delete the '.' from the **mc-leader-format**.

To use the print medium in a target:

1 Open a target.

2 Select the **Advanced** tab.

3 In the **Stylesheet Medium** field, select **print**.

Associating a topic with a stylesheet

Most projects use the same stylesheet for every topic. However, you can create multiple stylesheets and associate different stylesheets with specific topics.

Shortcut	Toolbar	Menu
F4 or Ctrl+Shift+P		Edit > Properties

To associate a topic with a stylesheet:

1 Open the Content Explorer or File List.

2 Right-click a topic and select **Properties**.

3 Select the **Topic Properties** tab.

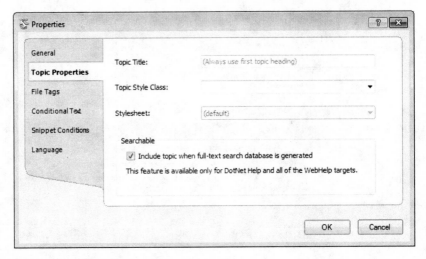

4   Select a stylesheet.

5   Click **OK**.
    The stylesheet is applied to the topic.

Associating multiple topics with a stylesheet

You probably don't want to individually associate each topic with your stylesheet. That could take a *long* time! If you want to use multiple stylesheets in a project, you can associate multiple topics with a stylesheet at the same time using the File List.

If you want to use the same stylesheet for every topic, see 'Associating all topics with a stylesheet' on page 170.

To associate multiple topics with a stylesheet:

1   Open the File List.
    If the File List is not open, select **View** > **File List**.

2   Filter the File List by **Topic Files**.

3   Select the topics.

4   Right-click the selected topics and select **Properties**.
    The Properties dialog box appears.

5 Select the **Topic Properties** tab.

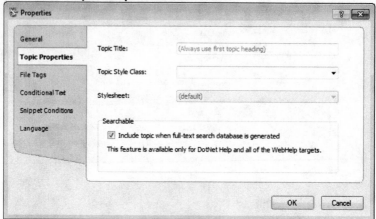

6 Select a **Stylesheet**.

7 Click **OK**.

The topics are associated with the stylesheet.

Associating all topics with a stylesheet

If you assign a master stylesheet to a project, every topic is automatically associated with the master stylesheet, including imported topics and any new topics you create in the future.

To associate all topics with a stylesheet:

1 Select **Project > Project Properties**.

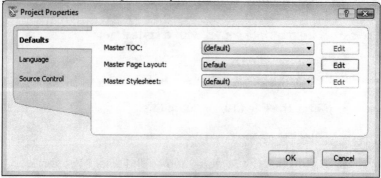

2 On the **Defaults** tab, select a **Master Stylesheet**.

3 Click **OK**.

Master pages

You can create a master page to include content at the top or bottom of topics in online targets, such as WebHelp. In addition to text, images, tables and other content, you can include the following dynamic elements (Flare calls these elements 'proxies') in a master page:

- **Breadcrumbs** automatically provide a list of the TOC books above the current topic. If your books are linked to topics, the links are included in the breadcrumb trail.

- A **mini-TOC** automatically adds links to the topics below the current topic.

'Is a master page the same as a RoboHelp template?'

Flare's master pages are very similar to RoboHelp's templates. However, Flare converts headers and footers in RoboHelp templates to snippets and insert the snippets into the topics that used the template. A snippet is content that you can reuse in your topics—not just in the header or footer. For more information about snippets, see page 197.

Creating a master page

You can create as many master pages as you need. Master pages have a .flmsp extension, and they are stored in the Resources\MasterPages folder in the Content Explorer.

Shortcut	Toolbar	Menu
Alt+P, M	none	Project > Add Master Page

To create a master page:

1 Select **Project** > **Add Master Page**.
The Add New Master Page dialog box appears.

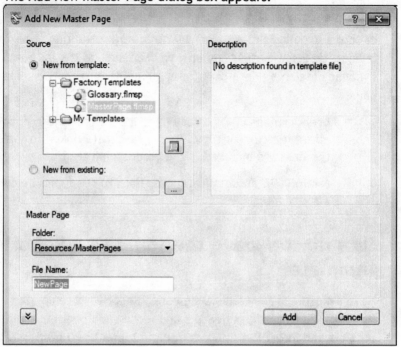

2 Select a **Source** template.

3 Type a **File name**.
Master pages have a .flmsp extension. If you don't type the extension, Flare will add it for you.

4 Click **Add**.
The Copy to Project dialog box appears.

5 Click **OK**.
The master page appears in the Content Explorer and opens in the XML Editor.

Adding content to a master page

You can add content to a master page above or below the topic body proxy.

Any content that you add above the topic body proxy will appear above the topic's content. However, it is not 'fixed' on the screen: it will scroll off the page in long topics.

Any content that you add below the topic body proxy will appear at the bottom of the topic. In long topics, users may need to scroll down to see it.

To add content to a master page:

1 Open the master page.

2 Position the cursor above or below the **topic body** proxy.

breadcrumbs proxy

]

topic body proxy

mini-toc proxy

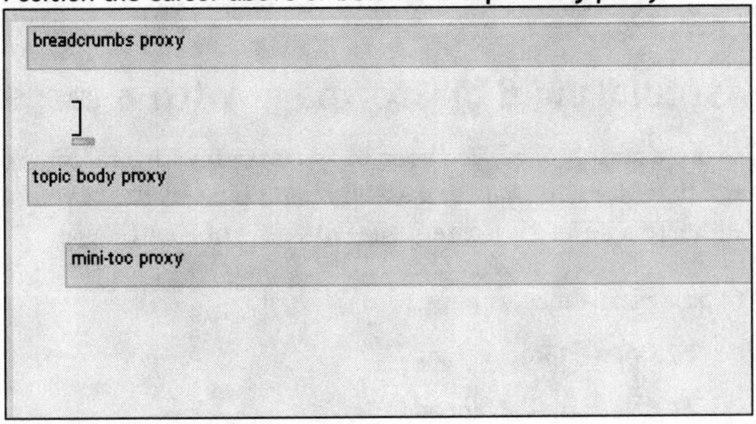

3 Type or insert your header's content.
You can add anything to a master page that you can add to a topic, including formatted content, images, lists, tables, variables, and snippets.

To add a proxy to a master page:

1 Open the master page.

2 Position the cursor above or below the **topic body** proxy.

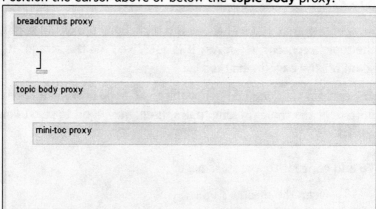

3 Select **Insert** > **Proxy** and select your proxy.

Associating a master page with a target

To use a master page, you need to associate it with a target. You can associate the same master page with multiple targets, or you can associate a different master page with each of your targets.

To associate a master page with a target:

1 Open a target.

2 Select the **Advanced** tab.

3 Select a **Master Page**.

4 Click **Save**.

Page layouts

You can create a page layout to set the page size and margins and to add headers and footers to print targets. You can add pages to a page layout to set up different headers and footers for first, title, odd, and even pages.

Creating a page layout

You can create multiple page layouts to apply different page sizes, margins, headers, or footers to different sections in a print target. For example, you can create a landscape page layout for wide tables or large graphics.

Page layouts have a .flpgl extension, and they are stored in the Resources\PageLayouts folder in the Content Explorer.

To create a page layout:

1   Select **Project** > **Add Page Layout**.
    The Add New Page dialog box appears.

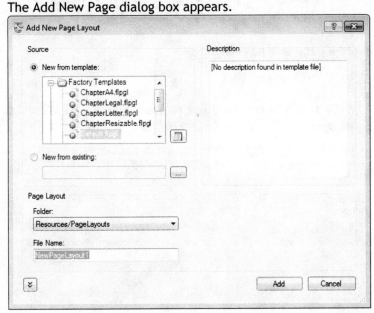

2 Select a **Source** template.

3 Type a **File Name**.

4 Click **Add**.
The page layout appears in the Page Layout Editor.

Adding pages to a page layout

You can include the following types of pages in a page layout:

- □ Title — often used for the first page in your TOC

- □ First — often used for the first page in a chapter as defined in your TOC

- □ Left — used for the left (even) pages in your print target

- □ Right — used for the right (odd) pages in your print target

- □ Empty — automatically inserted when needed if you set up chapters to start on right (odd) pages

TIP *If you are creating left and right pages for a Word target, you should also select the "Generate 'Mirror Margins' for M Word Output" option on the Advanced tab in your Word target.*

To add a page to a page layout:

1 Open a page layout.

2 In the Page Layout Editor toolbar, click [Page ▾] and select **Add Page**.
The new page appears.

3 Right-click the page and select **Page Properties**.
The Page Properties dialog box appears.

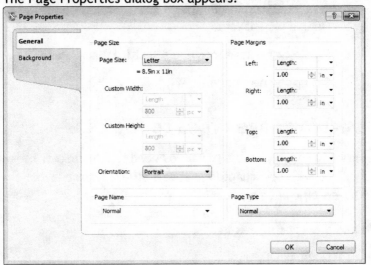

4 Select a **Page Type**.

5 Click **OK**.

Duplicating a page

1 Open a page layout.

2 Right-click a page icon and select **Duplicate Page**.

3 Set up the new page.

Assigning page types to topics

To assign a page type to a topic, you need to add chapter breaks in your TOC. Each new chapter can use a different page layout and start with a specific page type.

To add a chapter break in a TOC:

1 Open a TOC.

2 Right-click a TOC book or page and select **Properties**.
The Properties dialog box appears.

3 Select the **Printed Output** tab.

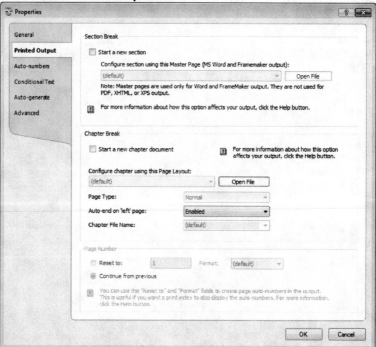

4 Select **Start a new chapter document**.

5 Select a **Page Layout**.

6 Select a **Page Type**.

7 Select whether you want the chapter to **Auto-end on 'left' page**.

8 Click **OK**.

Applying a page layout to a target

1 Open a target.

2 On the **General** tab, select a **Master Page Layout**.

Skins

Skins are used to format the toolbar and navigation pane and to set the size of the window for online targets. The WebHelp formats support the most customization options, followed by DotNet Help and HTML Help.

Skin files have a .flskn extension. They appear in the Skins folder in the Project Organizer.

'Is there a skin gallery?'

You can download and customize skins from MadCap's website at www.madcapsoftware.com/downloads/flareskingallery.aspx.

Creating a skin

You can use the same skin for all of your online targets, or you can create different skins for each target.

Shortcut	Toolbar	Menu
Alt+P, K	none	Project > Add Skin

To create a skin:

1 Select **Project** > **Add Skin**.
   —OR—
   Right-click the **Skins** folder and select **Add Skin**.

The Add Skin dialog box appears.

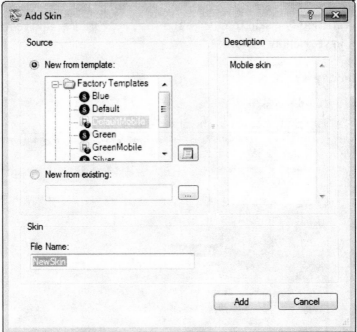

2   Select a **Source** template.

3   Type a **File Name**.
    Skins have a .flskn extension. If you don't type the extension,
    Flare will add it for you.

4   Click **Add**.
    The Copy to Project dialog box appears.

5   Click **OK**.
    The skin appears in the Skins folder in the Project Organizer
    and opens in the Skin Editor.

Modifying a skin

You can modify a skin to change the size, appearance, and features used in your online help.

To modify a skin:

1   Open the skin.
    The skin appears in the Skin Editor.

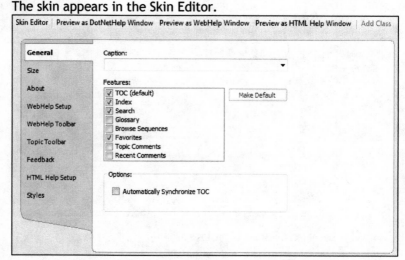

2   On the **General** tab, type a **Caption**.
    The caption appears in the WebHelp window's title bar.

3   Select the **Features** that you want to appear in the help window.

4   Enable or disable **Automatically Synchronize TOC**.

5   Select the **Size** tab.

6   If you want to specify a size for you help window:

    □   Deselect **Use Browser Default Size**.

    □   Type values for the window positions.
        —OR—
        Click **Preview Full Size**, resize the preview window, and click **OK**.

7 If you are editing a WebHelp skin:

- Select the **WebHelp Setup** tab.

- Type a **Navigation Pane Size**.
  If you type **0**, Flare will automatically size the navigation pane (the navigation pane is where the TOC, index, search, and other navigational features appear).

- Select a **Pane Position**.

- Select the number of **Visible Accordion Items** you would like to use (navigational features appear in an 'accordion,' similar to tabs). If you have selected more navigational features on the **General** tab than visible accordion items, the other items will appear as icons below the accordion.

- Select an **About Box Bitmap** image.
  The About box appears when the user clicks the logo on the far right of the toolbar.

- Select the **WebHelp Toolbar** tab.

- If you want to use a custom toolbar, select **Enable Custom Layout** and select the **WebHelp Toolbar Buttons** you want to include:

Button	Description
Add Topic to Favorites	Adds the current topic to the Favorites list.
Back	Opens the previously-viewed topic.
Collapse All	Collapses all toggler, drop-down, and expanding links in the current topic.
CurrentTopicIndex **NEW!**	The current topic's position in the browse sequence. For example, 'Page 2 of 5.'
EditUserProfile	Opens the Feedback Service Profile dialog box.
Expand All	Expands all toggler, drop-down, and expanding links in the current topic.

Button	Description
Forward	Opens the next topic (if the user has previously clicked the Back button).
Home	Opens the startup topic as specified on the Target's General tab.
NextTopic 【NEW】	Opens the next topic in the browse sequence.
PreviousTopic 【NEW】	Opens the previous topic in the browse sequence.
Print	Open the Print dialog box.
QuickSearch	Searches the current topic for a word or phrase.
Refresh	Reopens the current topic.
Remove Highlight	Turns off search highlighting.
Select Browse Sequence	Open the browse sequence in the navigation pane.
Select Favorites	Open the favorites list in the navigation pane.
Select Glossary	Opens the glossary in the navigation pane.
Select Index	Opens the index in the navigation pane.
SelectRecentComments	Opens the recent comments feedback pane.
Select Search	Opens the search in the navigation pane.
Select TOC	Opens table of contents in the navigation pane.
SelectTopicComments	Opens the topic comments feedback pane.
Separator	A dividing bar between buttons.
Stop	Cancels opening the topic.

Button	Description
Toggle Navigation Pane	Hides and shows the navigation pane.
Topic Ratings	Shows the topic rating icons (stars by default) that can be used to rate a topic

8 If you are editing an HTML Help skin:

- Click the **HTML Help Setup** tab.

- Select the **HTML Help Buttons** you want to include:

Button	Description
Hide	Hides and shows the navigation pane.
Locate	Highlights the current topic in the TOC.
Back	Opens the previously-viewed topic.
Forward	Opens the next topic (if the user has previously clicked the Back button).
Stop	Cancels opening the topic.
Refresh	Reopens the current topic.
Home	Opens the startup topic as specified on the Target's General tab.
Font	Increases the font size in topics.
Print	Open the Print dialog box.
QuickSearch	Searches the current topic.
Next	Opens the next topic in the TOC.
Previous	Opens the previous topic in the TOC.
Options	Opens a menu with the following commands: Home, Show, Back, Stop, Refresh, and Search Highlight On/Off.
Jump 1 and 2	Opens a specified website or topic (click Jump Button Options to select a target).

- Select the **Button, Navigation Pane,** and **Misc Options** you want to use.

TIP *To include the WebHelp toolbar (created on the WebHelp Toolbar tab) in HTML Help, select Display Toolbar in Each Topic.*

9   If you are editing a WebHelp skin, select the **Styles** tab and modify the styles as needed. You can change the font, icon, label, border, padding, and background settings for any toolbar item.

TIP *To change or remove the MadCap logo, open the ToolbarItem style group, select Logo, and change the Icon setting.*

10 Click **Save**.

Modifying a WebHelp mobile skin NEW

You can modify a WebHelp skin to change the size, appearance, and features used in your online help.

To modify a WebHelp mobile skin:

1   Open the skin.

The skin appears in the WebHelp Mobile Skin Editor.

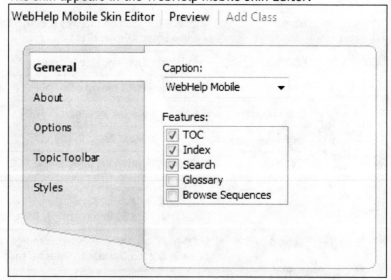

2 On the **General** tab, type a **Caption**.
The caption appears in the title bar.

3 Select the **Features** that you want to appear in the help window.

4 Select the **About** tab and select an **About Box Bitmap** image. The About box appears when the user clicks the logo on the far right of the toolbar.

5 Select the **Options** tab and select whether you want to display the number of sub-items inside a TOC or browse sequence book or the number of linked topics for an index entry.

6 Select the **Topic Toolbar** tab and select the **Toolbar Buttons** you want to include:

Button	Description
Collapse All	Collapses all toggler, drop-down, and expanding links in the current topic.
CurrentTopicIndex	The current topic's position in the browse sequence. For example, 'Page 2 of 5.'
Expand All	Expands all toggler, drop-down, and expanding links in the current topic.
NextTopic	Opens the next topic in the browse sequence.
PreviousTopic	Opens the previous topic in the browse sequence.

7 Select the **Styles** tab and modify the styles as needed. You can change the font, icon, label, border, padding, and background settings for any toolbar item.

8 Click **Save**.

Associating a skin with a target

To use a skin, you need to associate it with a target. You can associate the same skin with multiple targets, or you can associate different skins with each target.

To associate a skin with a target:

1 Open a target.

2 On the **General** tab, select a **Skin**.

3 Click **Save**.

Translating a skin

If you are using your skin for a WebHelp, WebHelp Plus, or WebHelp AIR target, Flare provides translated versions of the default labels and tool tips used for buttons, accordion items, and other skin elements.

If you are creating HTML Help, you cannot change these elements. Windows will automatically set the language.

To select a language for a WebHelp skin:

1 Open a target.

2 One the **Language** tab, select a language.

3 Click **Save**.

Sample questions for this section

1 What is inline formatting?
A) Formatting that is applied to a word or phrase rather than an entire block of content.
B) Formatting that is applied by highlighting content and changing its appearance.
C) 'Track changes' lines that automatically appear for new or modifed content.
D) Formatting that applies a strikethrough line to your content.

2 You should consider using a font set if you plan to create which format?
A) HTML Help
B) DotNet Help
C) WebHelp
D) PDF

3 If you select a master stylesheet, it is automatically assigned to which topics?
A) Existing topics
B) Imported topics
C) New topics you create after selecting the master stylesheet
D) All of the above

4 What is a breadcrumb?
A) The path to the current topic using the TOC.
B) The list of previous topics the user has viewed.
C) A way to mark a topic, like a favorite, so that it can be quickly found again.
D) A user comment about a topic.

5 How can you set different odd and even footers for a print target?
A) Create two master pages.
B) Create two page layouts.
C) Create a template with two master pages.
D) Create an odd and even page in a page layout.

6 Your skin includes 6 accordion items, but 'Visible Accordion Items' is set to 4. Where do the other 2 accordion items appear in your WebHelp?
A) They don't appear.
B) They all appear as accordion items.
C) They appear as icons below the accordion.
D) WebHelp uses tabs, not accordion items.

7 How do you apply a skin to a target?
A) Open the skin and select the target on the Targets tab.
B) Open the target and select the skin in the General tab.
C) Open the target and select the skin on the Skins tab.
D) Select Project Properties and select the skin as the Master Skin.

Single sourcing

This section covers:

- Variables
- Snippets
- Condition tags

Variables

A variable can only contain unformatted text. I often use variables for copyright statements and product names. If the copyright statement or product name changes, I just change my variable's definition and all of my topics are updated.

Flare also provides dynamic system and heading variables. System variables can be used to insert the date, time, page count, page number, and topic title. Heading variables can be used to insert the current heading (any level or a specific level). System and heading variables are often used in page layouts to set up headers and footers.

User-defined variables are stored in a variable set. You can create as many variable sets and variables as you need. Variable sets are stored in a file with a .flvar extension. They appear in the Variables folder in the Project Organizer.

Creating a variable set

You can create a new variable set to share variables between projects.

Shortcut	Toolbar	Menu
Alt+P, .	none	Project > Add Variable Set

To create a variable set:

1   Select **Project** > **Add Variable Set**.
    —OR—
    Right-click the Variables folder and select **Add Variable Set**.

The Add Variable Set dialog box appears.

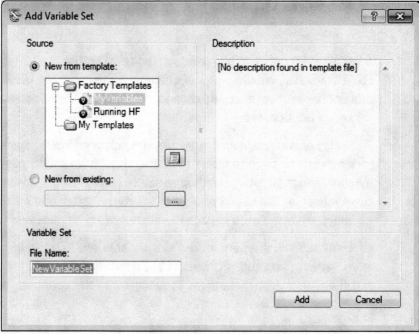

2 Select a **Source** template.

3 Type a **File Name**.

4 Click **Add**.

To create a variable:

1 Open the **Variables** folder in the Project Organizer.

2 Double-click a variable set.
The Variable Set Editor window appears.

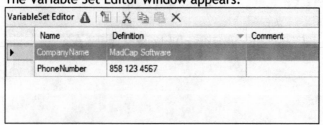

3 Click in the Variable Set Editor toolbar.

4 Type a name for the variable.

> *Be careful naming variables. If you rename a variable after you insert it into your topics, you will have to re-insert the variable into your topics.*

5 Type a definition for the variable.

To insert a variable:

1 Place your cursor where you want to insert the variable.

2 Select **Insert** > **Variable**.
The Variables dialog box appears.

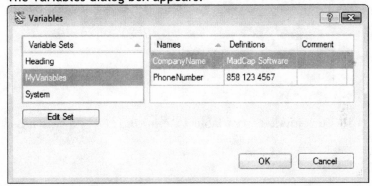

3 Select a variable set.

4 Select a variable.

5 Click **OK**.
The variable appears in the topic.

Overriding a variable's definition in a target

You can change a variable's definition when you create a target. If you change a variable's definition in the Target Editor, Flare will change the definition wherever you inserted the variable in your project.

To override a variable's definition:

1 Open the target.

2 Select the **Variables** tab.

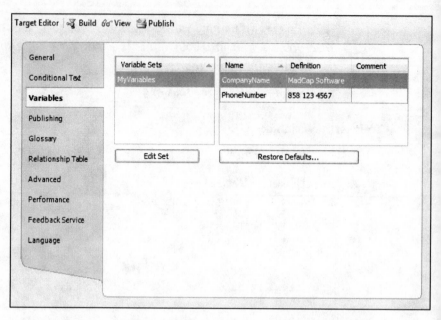

3 Click inside the variable's **Definition** cell and type a new value.

Snippets

A snippet can include any type of content, including formatted text, links, images, tables, lists, and variables. I often create snippets for tables and steps that I need to use in multiple topics.

Snippets are stored in a file with a .flsnp extension. They appear in the Resources\Snippets folder in the Content Explorer.

Creating a snippet using existing content

You can select content within a topic and convert it to a snippet.

Shortcut	Toolbar	Menu
Alt+O, E	none	Format > Create Snippet

To create a snippet using existing content:

1 Open the topic that contains the content you want to convert to a snippet.

2 Highlight the content you want to convert to a snippet.

3 Select **Format** > **Create Snippet**.
The Create Snippet dialog box appears.

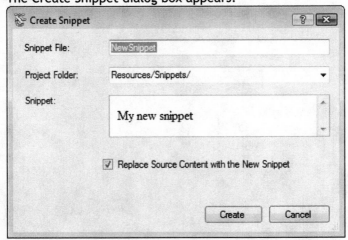

4 In the **Snippet File** field, type a new name for the snippet.

5 Leave the project folder selection as **Resources\Snippets**.

6 If you want the snippet to replace the highlighted text in the topic, select the **Replace Source Content with the New Snippet** option.

7 Click **Create**.
The snippet is created.

Creating a snippet using new content

You can also create a blank snippet and add content to it.

Shortcut	Toolbar	Menu
Alt+P, S	none	Project > Add Snippet

To create a snippet using new content:

1 Select **Project** > **Add Snippet**.
The Add New Snippet dialog box appears.

2   Select a **Source** template.

3   Select a **Folder**.
By default, snippets are stored in the Resources\Snippets folder.

4   Type a **File Name** for the snippet.

5   Click **Add**.
The Copy to Project dialog box appears.

6   Click **OK**.
The snippet appears in Content Explorer and opens in the XML Editor.

7   Click inside the snippet page in the XML Editor and add your content.

Inserting a snippet

You can insert snippets into topics, master pages, and page layouts.

Shortcut	Toolbar	Menu
Alt+I, N	none	Insert > Snippet

To insert a snippet to a topic:

1   Position the cursor where you want to insert the snippet.

2 Select **Insert > Snippet**.

The Insert Snippet Link appears.

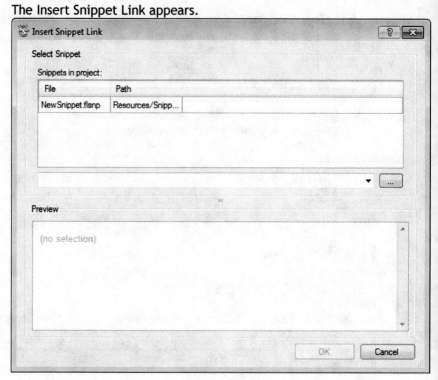

3 Select a snippet.

A preview of the snippet appears.

4 Click **OK**.

The snippet is added to the topic.

Condition tags

Condition tags can be used to include or exclude content when you create an online or print target. For example, you could create an 'External' tag and an 'Internal' tag to produce an external version of your help for customers and an internal version for the technical support department. Or, you could create a 'PrintOnly' tag to only include selected content when you create print documents. You can create as many condition tag sets and tags as you need.

You can apply a condition tag to almost anything: folders, topics, content in topics, TOC entries, index entries, stylesheets, variables, and snippets. Flare also makes it easier to specify which tags you want to include and exclude when you create a target.

Condition tags are stored in a condition tag set. When you import a RoboHelp project or FrameMaker document that contains conditional build tags, your tags are stored in a condition tag named after your import file.

TIP *If you insert an image created with MadCap Capture or insert a video created with MadCap Mimic into a Flare project, you can use your Flare project's condition tags in the image or video.*

Conditional tag sets have a .flcts extension. They appear in the Conditional Text folder in the Project Organizer.

'What are those boxes in the Content Explorer?'

They're called 'condition tag boxes.'

When you create a condition tag, you assign a color to the tag. This color is used to identify tagged content in a topic. If a folder or topic is associated with a tag, the condition tag box is filled with the tag's assigned color. If the folder or topic is associated with multiple tags, the condition tag box uses vertical stripes to show each tag's color.

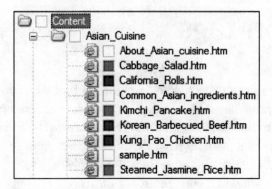

Creating a condition tag

To create a condition tag:

1 Open the Project Organizer.

2 Open the **Conditional Text** folder.

3 Double-click a condition tag set.
   The Condition Tag Set Editor appears.

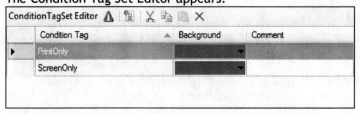

4 Click in the Condition Tag Set Editor toolbar.
   A new tag appears.

5 Double-click the new tag's name.

6 Type a new name for the tag and press **Enter**.

7 Select a color.

⚠ *Do not rename a tag after it is applied to topics or content.
   Flare will not update the tagged content to use the new
   name, so you will have to reapply the tag to everything.*

Applying a tag to content in a topic

To apply a tag to content in a topic:

1 Open a topic.

2 Select the content to be tagged.
You can apply a tag to any content, including characters, words, paragraphs, table columns/rows, and images.

3 Select **Format** > **Conditions**.
The Condition Tags dialog box appears.

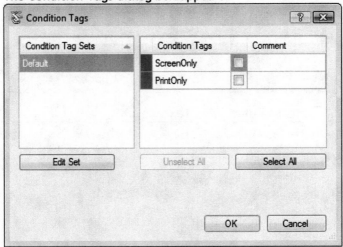

4 Select a condition tag's checkbox.

5 Click **OK**.
The tag is applied. The tagged content is shaded using the tag's color.

Applying a tag to a topic, file, or folder

To apply a tag to a topic, file, or folder:

1 Open the Content Explorer.

2 Select the topic, file, or folder to be tagged.

3 Click 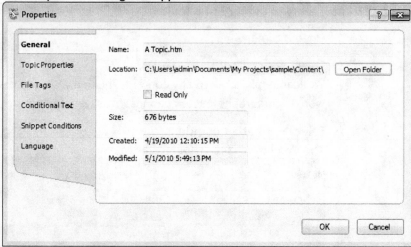 in the Content Explorer toolbar.

The Properties dialog box appears.

4 Select the **Conditional Text** tab.

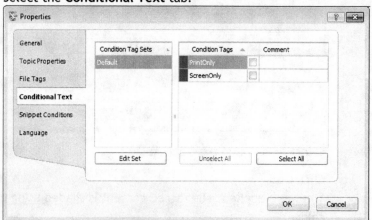

5 Select a condition tag's checkbox.

6 Click **OK**.

The tag is applied and the file or folder's condition tag box is filled with the tag's color.

Applying a tag to a TOC book or page

To apply a tag to a TOC book or page:

1 Open the Project Organizer.

2 Double-click a TOC.

3 Select a book or page and click 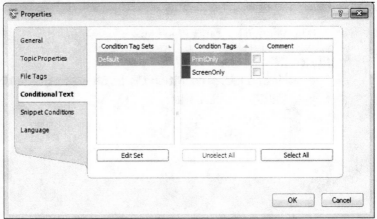 in the TOC Editor.
The Properties dialog box appears.

4 Select the **Conditional Text** tab.

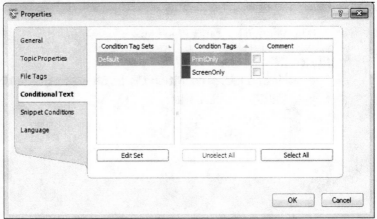

5 Select a condition tag's checkbox.

6 Click **OK**.
The tag is applied and the Toc book or page's condition tag box
is filled with the tag's color.

Applying a tag to an index entry

To apply a tag to an index entry:

1 Open a topic.

2 Select an index entry marker.

3 Select **Format > Conditions**.
The Condition Tags dialog box appears.

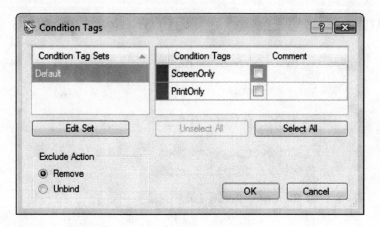

4 Select a condition tag's checkbox.

5 Click **OK**.

The tag is applied. A condition tag box appears inside the tagged index entry's marker.

Sample questions for this section

1 Where are variables stored?
A) In variable sets in the Project Organizer
B) In variable files in the Content Explorer's Resources folder
C) In variable files in the Content Explorer's Variables folder
D) Inside topics

2 A variable's definition can be set: (select all that apply)
A) Inside a topic
B) In the VariableSet Editor
C) In a target on the Variables tab
D) In the Project Properties on the Variables tab

3 A snippet can contain: (select all that apply)
A) Formatted text
B) Tables
C) Lists
D) Variables

4 Where are snippets are stored?
A) In snippet sets in the Project Organizer
B) In snippet files in the Content Explorer
C) In snippet files in the Content Explorer
D) Inside topics

5 A condition tag can be applied to: (select all that apply)
A) Topics
B) Folders
C) TOC books and pages
D) Index keywords

6 What happens if you rename a condition tag after it has been applied to content?
A) Flare automatically updates the content to use the new condition tag name.
B) Flare asks if you want to update the content to use the new name.
C) The condition tag is removed from your content.
D) Nothing—you must update the content yourself to use the new name.

7 Condition tags can be applied to the following targets (select all that apply):

A) PDF

B) Word

C) HTML Help

D) WebHelp

Publishing

This section covers:

- Targets
- Context-sensitive help

Targets

You can create eleven types of online help and print document targets from Flare. Each target type is summarized in the tables below.

Online targets

Target	Description
DITA	A 'code' format that creates DITA-based topics and a DITA map. These files can be integrated into another application or a content-management system ('CMS').
DotNet Help	An online format developed by MadCap Software that can be used to create Windows-based help for .NET applications. DotNet Help runs in the MadCap Help Viewer, and DotNet Help systems have a .mchelp file extension.
HTML Help	An online format developed by Microsoft that can be used to create Windows-based help. Microsoft no longer maintains or supports the HTML Help format, and they have promised an eventual replacement. HTML Help systems run in the HTML Help Viewer and they have a .chm (often pronounced 'chum') file extension.
WebHelp	An online format developed by MadCap Software that can be used to create Web-based help. WebHelp runs in a browser, so it is non Windows-specific like DotNet Help and HTML Help.
WebHelp Mobile **NEW!**	An special version of WebHelp that was designed to be viewed on handheld devices such as iPhones.
WebHelp Plus	A special version of WebHelp that provides faster searches and allows users to search content in .pdf, .doc, and .xls files. Unlike WebHelp, WebHelp Plus requires a Microsoft Web server with IIS.
WebHelp AIR	A special version of WebHelp that can be run locally rather than from a Web server. WebHelp AIR requires Adobe AIR, and WebHelp AIR help systems have a .air file extension.

'What is DITA?'

DITA stands for 'Darwin Information Typing Architecture.' It was created by IBM, but it is now a standard of the Organization for the Advancement of Structured Information Standards (OASIS).

'What is DotNet Help?'

MadCap's DotNet Help is a new format that was designed to be used with .NET applications. It is similar to WebHelp, but it runs inside the freely distributable MadCap Help viewer.

HTML Help cannot run from a file server because Microsoft has disabled the format for 'security reasons.'

WebHelp cannot run locally or from a file server in Internet Explorer because Microsoft blocks 'active content.' Users can enable active content in Internet Explorer, but you will need to provide instructions.

TIP *To enable active content in Internet Explorer, open Internet Explorer, select **Tools > Options**, click **Advanced**, and turn on **Allow active content to run in files on My Computer**.*

'What about WinHelp?'

Flare cannot create WinHelp. Microsoft's WinHelp is an old help format that was replaced by HTML Help. Microsoft has been phasing out WinHelp for over ten years, and they stopped officially supporting it with Windows Vista.

'Is Flare's WebHelp the same as RoboHelp's WebHelp?'

Flare's version of WebHelp looks very different from RoboHelp's WebHelp. Flare's WebHelp uses an accordion to display the TOC, index, search, and glossary.

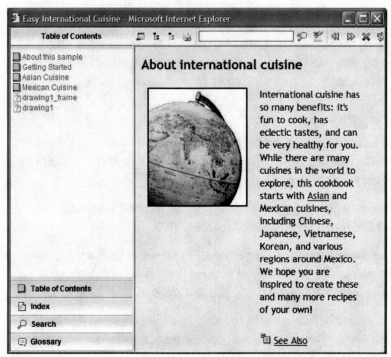

Flare's WebHelp

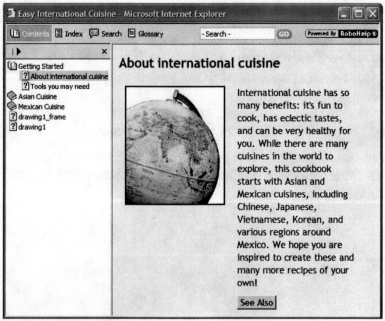

RoboHelp's WebHelp

Print targets

Target	Description
FrameMaker document	A print format that creates Adobe FrameMaker .book and .fm documents.
PDF document	A print format developed by Adobe. The PDF format combines all of your topics and images into one file with a .pdf ('Portable Document Format') extension.
Word document	A print format that creates Microsoft .doc or .docx documents.
XHTML document	A print and online format that combines all of your topics into one file with a .xhtml file extension.
XPS document	A print format developed by Microsoft. XPS is similar to Adobe's PDF format, but it is based on XML. XPS combines all of your topics into one file with a .xps ('XML Paper Specification') extension.

'What is XPS?'

XPS stands for 'XML Paper Specification.' It was created by Microsoft, but it has been released under a royalty-free copyright license. An XPS Document package should appear the same on any computer. The two main differences between the PDF and XPS formats are that an XPS Document package is a .zip file (with a .xps extension instead of .zip), and XPS is based on XML.

Creating a target

You should create a different target for each version of your online help or print documents. For example, if you need to create WebHelp and print documentation for the 'Standard' and 'Professional' versions of your product, you should create four targets.

Shortcut	Toolbar	Menu
Alt+P, R	none	Project > Add Target

To create a target:

1 Select **Project** > **Add Target**.
   —OR—
   Right-click the Targets folder and select **Add Target**.

   The Add New Item dialog box appears.

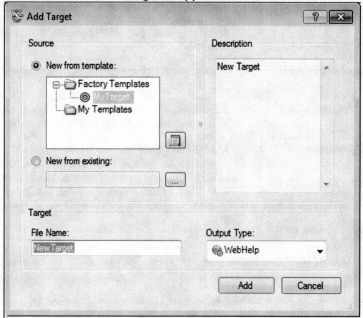

2 Select a **Source** template.

3 Type a **File Name**.
   You don't have to type the .fltar extension. Flare will add it for
   you if you leave it out.

4 Select an **Output Type**.

5 Click **Add**.
   The target appears in the Targets folder in the Project
   Organizer and opens in the Target Editor.

Specifying the primary target

The primary target is the target that you plan to create the most often. When you preview a topic, the topic will appear as it will appear in the primary target.

To specify the primary target:

- Right-click a target and select **Make Primary**.

Setting up an online target

You can specify the skin, master page, TOC, condition tags, variables, and glossaries that are used in your online target.

To set up an online target:

1 Open the target.

2 On the **General** tab, select the following options:

- **Output Type** — the help format that you are creating.

- **Comment** — a short description of the target.

- **Startup Topic** — the first topic that appears when the user opens your help system.

- **Skin** — the skin file specifies the size, appearance, and features included in a target.

- **Master TOC** — the TOC that will be used for the target.

- **Browse Sequence** — the browse sequence that will be used for the target.

- **Master Page Layout** — the page layout that will be used for all topics in a print target. Setting the master page layout will override page layouts that have been applied to specific topics.

- **Master Stylesheet** — the stylesheet that will be used for all topics. Setting the master stylesheet will override stylesheets that have been applied to specific topics.

- ◻ **Output File** — the name of the main entry (or 'start') file for your help system.

- ◻ **Output Folder** — where the generated help files will be created.

3 Select the **Conditional Text** tab.

4 Select whether you want to include or exclude each tag.

5 Select the **Variables** tab.

6 If you need to change a variable's definition for the target, click inside its **Definition** cell and type a new value.

7 If you want to publish your online help to a file or web server:

- ◻ Select the **Publishing** tab.

- ◻ Select a destination.
  —OR—
  Click **New Destination** to create a publishing destination.

8 Select the **Glossary** tab and select the following options:

- ◻ **Glossary Term Conversion** method — how your glossary terms are converted in your topics.

- ◻ **Glossary** — the glossary (or glossaries) that are included in your target.

9 If you are using relationship tables and links, select the **Relationship Table** tab and select the relationship tables to use in your target.

10 Select the **Advanced** tab and select the options you would like to use. Commonly-set options include:

- ◻ **Insert Mark of the Web** — select to avoid Internet Explorer's 'active content' error message when you open your WebHelp files locally.

- ◻ **Master Page** — select a master page to apply to your topics.

11 If you are building a large 8,000+ topic DotNet Help, WebHelp, or WebHelp Plus target, select the **Performance** tab and select the following options:

- **Index** — pre-merging the index file and using smaller index 'chunks' can make the index open faster for the user.

- **TOC** — using smaller TOC chunks can make the TOC open faster for the user.

- **Search Database** — you can exclude non-words from search (such as code examples), pre-merge the search or using smaller search chunks to make the search open faster for the user, and use larger n-grams to make a Japanese, Chinese, or Korean language search more accurate.

12 If you are using MadCap Feedback, select the **Feedback Service** tab, select the **Enable Feedback Service** option, and enter your license key.

13 If you are creating a WebHelp target, select the **Language** tab and select a language for the skin.

14 Click **Save**.

Setting up a print target NEW!

You can create a print target to specify the condition tags, variables, and glossaries that are used in your print documentation. Flare 6 includes a new PDF Output tab that can be used to set advanced PDF options.

To set up a print target:

1 Open the target.

2 On the **General** tab, select the following options:

- **Output Type** — the help format that you are creating.

- **Comment** — a short description of the target.

- **Master TOC** — the TOC that will be used for the target.

- **Master Page Layout** — the page layout that will be used for all topics in a print target. Setting the master page layout will override page layouts that have been applied to specific topics.

- **Master Stylesheet** — the stylesheet that will be used for all topics. Setting the master stylesheet will override stylesheets that have been applied to specific topics.

- **Output File** — the name of the generated document.

  TIP▷ *To create a Word 2007 document, include the .docx extension.*

- **Output Folder** — where the generated files will be created.

3 Select the **Conditional Text** tab.

4 Select whether you want to include or exclude each tag.

5 Select the **Variables** tab.

6 If you need to change a variable's definition for the target, click inside its Definition cell and type a new value.

7 If you want to publish your print document to a file or web server:

- Select the **Publishing** tab.

- Select a destination.
  —OR—
  Click **New Destination** to create a publishing destination.

8 Select the **Glossary** tab and select a **Glossary** (or glossaries) to include in your documentation.

9 If you are using relationship tables and links, select the **Relationship Table** tab and select the relationship tables to use in your target.

10 Select the **Advanced** tab and select the options you would like to use. The most commonly-set option is:

- **Stylesheet Medium** — if your stylesheet contains a medium (most people use the 'print' medium), you can use the medium's styles or the stylesheet's default styles.

- **Expanding Text Effects** — select how expanding text should appear in your print documents.

- **Text Popup Effects** — select how text popups should appear in your print document.

- **Generated TOC** — select whether your heading levels should match your TOC or the heading tags you used in your topics. Also, select whether you want to create headings for unlinked books in your TOC.

- **Multi-Document Native XPS/PDF Output** — if you are creating a PDF or XPS document, select this option to create multiple documents based on chapter breaks in the TOC. See 'Specifying Chapter Breaks' on page 131.

- **Generate Multiple Documents for MS Word Output** — if you are creating a Word document, select this option to create multiple documents based on chapter breaks in the TOC. See 'Specifying Chapter Breaks' on page 131.

- Redacted Text — if you are using the redacted style property, you can set how it will appear in your print target.

11 If you are creating a PDF target, click **PDF Options** and select the following options:

- **Image Compression** — set the **Compression** option to **Automatic** to use Flare's lossless compression for non-JPG images or select **JPG** to convert all images to JPGs with some compression.

- **Document Properties** — type a title, author, subject, and any keywords you want to include.

- **Initial View** — select the magnification level to use when opening the document and whether the Bookmarks panel should appear.

□ **Security** – select whether you want to require a password or if you want to restrict the user from printing, editing, or copying text and graphics.

12 Click **Save**.

Building a target

By default, your generated targets are stored in a folder named 'Outputs.' You can change the default folder, but most users use the default folder.

Shortcut	Toolbar	Menu
F6	Build Primary ▾	Build > Build Primary

To build a target:

1 Click the down arrow beside the Build Primary ▾ icon and select a target.
—OR—
Right-click a target and select **Build**.

2 If you made any changes to the target, Flare will prompt you to save your changes. Click **Yes**.
The Build Progress dialog box appears.

3 When the build is complete, click **Yes** to view the generated target.

TIP▷ *You can select* **Build** > **Clean Project** *to delete everything in the Output folder.*

Building a target from the command line

Flare targets can be compiled from the command line. This feature can be used to build your targets from a batch file when you compile an application.

To build a target from the command line:

1 Open a command prompt.

2 Navigate to the directory where you installed Flare. The default directory for Flare 5 is program files\madcap software\madcap flare v5\flare.app.

3 Type **madbuild -project <path><projectname> -target <targetname>**. For example:

```
madbuild -project c:\myFolder\myProject.flprj
-target myWebHelp
```

To build all of your targets from the command line:

1 Open a command prompt.

2 Navigate to the directory where you installed Flare. The default directory for Flare 5 is program files\madcap software\madcap flare v5\flare.app.

3 Type **madbuild -project <path><projectfilename>**. For example: `madbuild -project c:\myFolder\myProject.flprj`

Batch generating targets NEW!

You can create a batch target to build and/or publish multiple targets. You can even schedule a batch target to run at a specific time every day, week, or month.

To create a batch generate target:

1 Select **Project > Add Batch Target**.
—OR—
Right-click the Targets folder and select **Add Batch Target**.

The Add Batch Target dialog box appears.

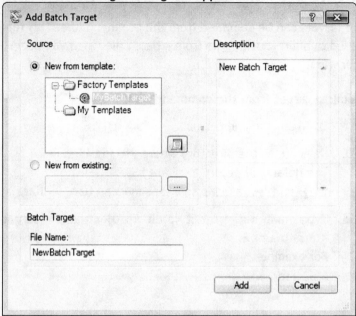

2 Select a **Source** template.

3 Type a **File Name**.
You don't have to type the .fltar extension. Flare will add it for you if you leave it out.

4 Click **Add**.
The batch target appears in the Targets folder in the Project Organizer and opens in the Target Editor.

5 On the **Targets** tab, select the target(s) you want to build and/or publish.

6 Click **Save**.

To schedule a batch generate target:

1 Open a batch target.

2 Select the **Schedule** tab.

3 Click **New**.

The New Trigger dialog box appears.

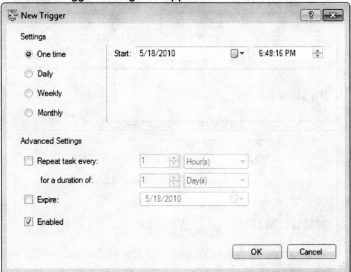

4 Select a frequency **Setting**.

5 Select a **Start** date and time.

6 If you selected a daily, weekly, or monthly frequency setting, select the recurrence details.

7 If the batch generate should repeat, select **Repeat task every** and specify how often and how long the repeating should occur.

8 If the repeating should expire, select **Expire** and specify an expiration date.

9 If you are ready to enable the batch generate, select **Enable**.

10 Click **OK**.

Viewing a target

Shortcut	Toolbar	Menu
Shift+F6	*View Primary* ▾	Build > View Primary

To view a target:

- Click the down arrow beside the *View Primary* ▾ icon and select a target.
  —OR—
  Right-click a target and select **View**.

Publishing a target

You can publish any target to a file server or an FTP server. If you create multiple publishing destinations, you can publish to multiple destinations at the same time.

Shortcut	Toolbar	Menu
Ctrl+F6		Build > Publish Primary

To create a publishing destination:

1 Open a target.

2 Select the **Publishing** tab.

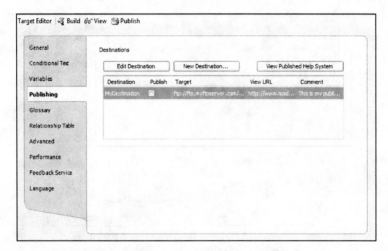

3 Click **New Destination**.

The Add New Item dialog box appears.

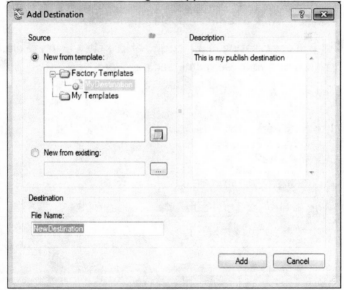

4 Select a **Source** template.

5 Type a **File Name**.

6 Click **Add**.

The destination appears in the Destinations folder in the Project Organizer and opens in the Destination Editor.

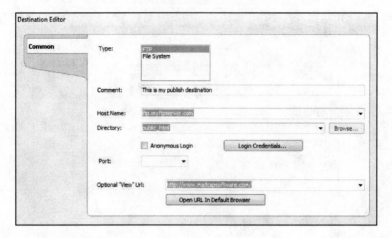

7 Select a destination type.

8 Type a **Comment**.

9 Click **Browse** to select a publishing directory.

10 If you are creating an FTP destination, click **Login Credentials** to provide your user name and password.

11 Click **Save**.

To publish a target:

1 Open a target.

2 Click .

The Publishing Target dialog box appears.

3 Select one (or more) of the publishing destinations.

4 Select **Upload Only Changed Files** to only republished files that have changed.

5 Select **Remove Stale Files** to remove files from the server that have been removed from your project.

6 Click **Start Publishing**.
Flare copies the generated files to the publishing destination.

Context-sensitive help

Context-sensitive help (or 'CSH' if you like acronyms) is help that opens to a specific topic based on where you are in an application. For example, a 'Print Preview' dialog box would open a help topic about printing, and a 'Save' dialog box would open a topic about saving a file.

To create context-sensitive help, you need to associate your help topics to the windows and dialog boxes that are used in your application. This process is called 'mapping,' and it uses two files: header files and alias files.

Adding a header file

A header file is used to assign a number and an identifier to each dialog box and window in an application. Many programming applications create header files automatically, but you can also create header files using Flare. Header files have a .h or .hh extension, and they appear in the Advanced folder in the Project Organizer.

Header files use the following format:
```
#define MyID number
```

For example:
```
#define Save_dialog 1000
```

Shortcut	Toolbar	Menu
Alt+P, V, H	none	Project > Advanced > Add Header File

To create a header file:

If your software team has created a header file, you can copy it to the Advanced folder in the Project folder. If you need to create a header file, follow these steps.

1 Select **Project > Advanced > Add Header File.**
   The Add Header File dialog box appears.

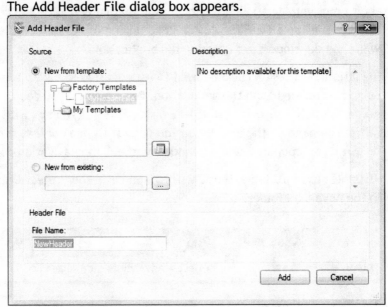

2 Select a **Source** template.

3 Type a **File Name** for the header file.
   You don't have to type the .h extension. Flare will add it for you if you leave it out.

4 Click **Add.**
   The header file appears in the Advanced folder in the Project Organizer and opens in the Text Editor.

Creating an alias file

Alias files are used to match identifiers to a help topic. At first, an alias file might seem unnecessary: why not just put everything in the header file? The reason is that you need to share the header file with the development team. They need it to compile the application, and their programming application might automatically update the header file. By using an alias file, you can keep linking topics to identifiers while the developers are creating the application.

In Flare, alias files can also be used to assign a skin to a help topic when it is opened from the application. For example, you could normally open your help system in a large, 700x500 window with the navigation pane on the left. When you open it from a context-sensitive link, it could open in a smaller window without the navigation pane.

Alias files have a .flali extension. They appear in the Project Organizer in the Advanced folder.

Shortcut	Toolbar	Menu
Alt+P, V, L	none	Project > Advanced > Add Alias File

To create an alias file:

1 Select **Project>Advanced>Add Alias File**.
The Add Alias File dialog box appears.

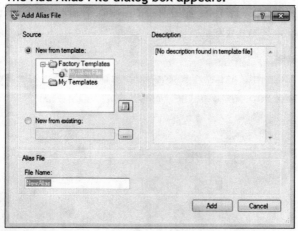

2   Select a **Source** template.

3   Type a **File Name** for the alias file.
    You don't have to type the .flali extension. Flare will add it for
    you if you leave it out.

4   Click **Add**.
    The alias file appears in the Advanced folder in the Project
    Organizer and opens in the Alias Editor.

To assign an identifier to a topic:

1   Open the alias file.
    Alias files are stored in the Advanced folder in the Project
    Organizer.

2   On the left side of the Alias Editor, select an identifier.

3   On the right side of the Alias Editor, select a topic to link to
    the identifier.

4   If you want to use a skin when opening the topic, select the
    skin.

5   Click **Assign**.
    The topic's filename appears in the **Topic** column.

6   Continue assigning topics to Identfiers.

7   Save your alias file.
    You can open your alias file and add new identifiers at any
    time.

Testing context-sensitive help

After you assign identifiers to your topics, you can test your context-
sensitive help links.

To test your context-sensitive help:

1   Build your target.

2   Right-click your target and select **Test CSH API Calls**.
    The Context-sensitive Help API Tester dialog box appears.

3 Next to each identifier, click Test .
The correct help topic should appear.

4 When you are finished testing, click **Close**.

Sample questions for this section

1 Which output types were created by MadCap software? (select all that apply)
   A) DotNet Help
   B) HTML Help
   C) WebHelp
   D) XPS

2 How can you set up your WebHelp to not display the 'Active Content' message?
   A) Select **Tools** > **Options** and select **Disable Active Content**.
   B) Select **Disable Active Content** in your target.
   C) Select **Mark of the Web** in your target.
   D) It should not appear for WebHelp. It only appears in HTML Help.

3 What is a primary target?
   A) The main or "master" target in merged projects.
   B) The only target you can create from a project.
   C) A project you plan to link to another project.
   D) The target you expect to build the most often.

4 How many targets can you set up in a project?
   A) One
   B) One for each type (i.e., one HTML Help, one WebHelp, etc)
   C) One for online and one for print.
   D) As many as you want.

5 What happens when you select **Build** > **Clean Project**?
   A) Flare fixes any incorrect XHTML code in your topics.
   B) Flare finds any files in the Content folder that are not being used.
   C) Flare deletes everything in the Output folder.
   D) Flare fixes any broken links.

6 What happens when you publish a target?
   A) Flare creates the output files.
   B) Flare copies the output files to a network or a website.
   C) Flare prints the output files.
   D) Flare creates a postscript file that you can send to a printer.

7 What is the "startup" topic?

A) The topic that opens when you open the project in Flare.

B) The first topic that users see when they open the online target.

C) The file users double-click to open the target.

D) The file you double-click to open your project in Flare.

Project management

This section covers:

- Topic templates
- File tags
- Reports
- Annotations
- Topics reviews
- Feedback
- Source control

Topic templates NEW!

Everything you create in Flare, including topics, stylesheets, master pages, and page layouts, is based on a template. Templates are just a "starting point" when you create a file. For example, a new topic is simply a copy of the template that you use. The new topic is not linked to the template.

Creating a topic template

If your topics always have a similar structure, such as a heading, paragraph, table, and list, you can create a template to start your topics with these blocks of content.

Shortcut	Toolbar	Menu
Alt+F, M	none	File > Save as Template

To create a topic template:

1   Open the topic that you want to become a template.

2   Select **File** > **Save as Template**.
    The Save as Template dialog box appears.

3   Type a **Template Name**.

4   Click **OK**.
    Your template will be available in the My Templates folder.

TIP▷ *By default, templates are stored in the "My Templates" folder. This folder is actually the My Documents\My Templates\Content folder on your PC. If you work on a team, you can move your templates to a file server. When you create a new topic, select "New from existing" and click* ⌐...⌐ *to select the template on the file server.*

File Tags and Reports 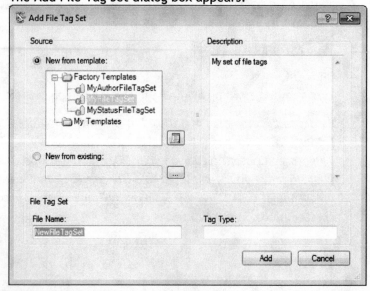NEW!

You can create file tags to specify authors, status levels, or any other type information for files in your project. For example, you could create a "reviewer" tag to track who the subject-matter expert reviewer should be for each topic. File tags can be assigned to any type of file in your project.

Creating a file tag set

Flare provides templates to create author and status file tags, and you can modify them as needed. Or, you can create your own file tag set.

Shortcut	Toolbar	Menu
Alt+P, V, F	none	Project > Advanced > Add File Tag Set

To create a file tag set:

1 Select **Project** > **Advanced** > **Add File Tag Set**.
The Add File Tag Set dialog box appears.

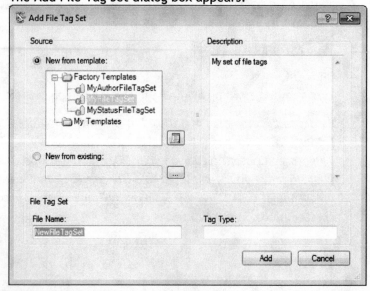

2 Select a **Source** template.

3 Type a **File Name**.

4 Click **Add**.
The file tag set file appears in the Advanced folder in the Project Organizer and opens in the File Tag Set Editor.

To add a tag to a file tag set:

1 Open a file tag set.

2 Click .
The new tag appears.

3 Type a name for the tag.

To apply a tag:

1 Right-click a file and select **Propeprties**.
The Properties dialog box appears.

2 Select the **File Tag** tab.

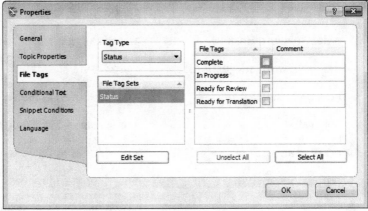

3 Select a **Tag Type**.

4 Select a **File Tag**.

5 Click **OK**.

Creating a report

You can create reports based on your file tags, or you can create report that include any of the following information:

- absolute links
- assigned CSH IDs
- broken bookmarks
- broken links
- concept links
- database errors
- duplicate CSH map IDs
- duplicate styles
- duplicate TOCitems
- external links
- files with tags
- index feyword links
- index feyword suggestions
- new style suggestions
- non-XML topics
- project annotations
- replace local style suggestions
- snippet suggestions
- TOC - primary target
- topics linked by CSH map ID
- topics not in index

- topics not In TOC
- topics not linked
- topics not linked By map ID
- topics with images
- undefined condition tags
- undefined file tags
- undefined glossary term links
- undefined styles
- undefined variables
- used concepts
- used index keywords
- used language tags
- used style sheets
- used/unused condition tags
- used/unused content files
- used/unused CSH IDs
- used/unused limages
- used/nused multimedia
- used/unused styles
- used/unused variables
- variable suggestions

Shortcut	Toolbar	Menu
Alt+P, F	none	Project > Add Report File

To create a report file:

1 Select **Project** > **Add Report File**.
   —OR—
   Right-click the Reports folder and select **Add Report File**.
   The Add Report dialog box appears.

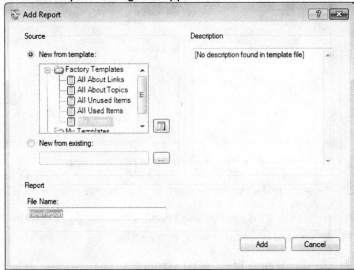

2 Select a **Source** template.

3 Type a **File Name**.

4 Click **Add**.
   The file tag set file appears in the Reports folder in the Project
   Organizer and opens in the Report Editor.

To generate, save, or print a report:

1 Open a report.

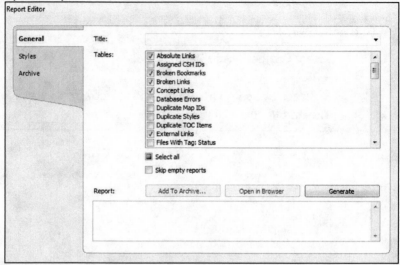

2 On the **General** tab, type a **Title** for the report.

3 Select the **Tables** to include in the report.

4 If you want to change the report's formatting, click the **Styles** tab and changes the style properties.

5 On the **General** tab, click **Generate**.

6 To print or save the report, click **Open in Browser**.

Annotations and topic reviews

You can add annotations to your topics to keep notes or to track your development progress. If you send topics for review, reviewers can use X-Edit Review to add annotations. Annotations are not included when you build a target.

Adding an annotation

You can add an annotation anywhere in a topic, and you can add as many annotations as you need.

Shortcut	Toolbar	Menu
none	Insert Annotation	Insert > Insert Annotation

To add an annotation:

1 Open a topic.

2 Select the content that you would like to annotate.

3 Select **Insert** > **Insert Annotation**.
   The Edit Annotation Pane appears.

4 If this is your first annotation, type your initials.

5 Type your annotation.

To show or hide annotations:

1 Open a topic.

2 If the Review toolbar is not open, select **View** > **Toolbars** > **Review**.

3 Click Show Annotations .

Locking content

You can lock content so that it cannot be edited. For example, you might lock a paragraph so that a reviewer using X-Edit can see it but not change it.

To lock content so that it cannot be edited:

1 Open a topic.

2 Position your cursor inside the content you want to lock.

3 Select **Format > Locks > Mark Element(s) to be Locked**.

4 Select **Format > Locks > Locks (Disabled)**.
   The paragraphs are locked and cannot be edited.

Sending topics for review NEW!

In Flare 6, you can create a review package to send multiple topics for review. Reviewers can use X-Edit Review to add annotations. If a reviewer is using the full version of X-Edit (and you enable topic editing when you send the topic), reviewers can also edit the topic.

To send topics for review:

1 If the Review toolbar is not open, select **View > Toolbars > Review**.

2 Click Send For Review... .
   The Send Topic for Review dialog box appears.

3 Type a **Review Package Name**.

4 Click **Add Topics**.
   The Open File dialog box appears.

5 Select the topics you want to send for review and click **Open**.

6 If you want to allow reviewers to edit the topic, select **Allow reviewers to edit content**.

7 Click **Next**.

8 Type a subject and message for the email.

9 Click **Add Email Recipient** to select a recipient.

10 Click **Send**.
Your email application will open.

11 Send the email.

To view a list of topics that have been sent for review:

1 Select **File** > **Review** > **Topic Reviews**.

2 In the text box at the top of the window, select **Sent Topics**.

Accepting an annotation

If you accept a reviewer's annotations, they are added to your topic and appear in the Annotations pane. You can accept individual annotations or all of the annotations in a topic.

To accept an annotation:

1 Open a topic.

2 Select **File** > **Review** > **Topic Reviews**.

3 In the text box at the top of the window, select **Inbox**.

4 Select a topic.

5 Click Accept Annotations... .
The Accept Annotations dialog box appears.

6 Select the annotations you want to accept.

7 Click **OK**.

Accepting a reviewed topic

If you allow reviewers to edit a topic using X-Edit, you can accept the reviewed topic. When you accept the reviewed topic, the original topic is replaced by the reviewed topic.

To accept reviewed topics:

1 Select **File** > **Review** > **Topic Reviews.**

2 In the text box at the top of the window, select **Inbox.**

3 Select a topic.

4 Click Accept Topic... and click **OK.**

Feedback

You can use MadCap Feedback to add user comments and topic reviews to WebHelp, WebHelp Plus, HTML Help, and DotNet Help. Feedback can also be used to review users' search terms and a list of topics that have been opened using context-sensitive help.

You can either purchase and install Feedback Server on your web server, or you can purchase MadCap Feedback Service and MadCap will host the comments and ratings data on their server. Feedback Server requires a Microsoft Windows-based web server.

Enabling user comments

You can set up a skin to display user comments at the bottom of your topics. For WebHelp and WebHelp Plus, you can also display user comments in a Topic Comments pane.

To enable user comments:

1 Open a skin.
   The Skin Editor appears.

2 Select the **General** tab.

3 Select **Topic Comments**.

4 If you want to allow users to view the most recent comments, select **Recent Comments**.

5 If you want to display the topic comments at the bottom of your topics, select **Display topic comments at the end of each topic**.

   ◇ *This option is only supported by WebHelp and WebHelp Plus.*

6 Save the skin.

To enable feedback for a target:

1 Open a target.

2 Select the **Feedback Service** tab.

3 Select **Enable Feedback Service**.

4 In the **Feedback Server URL** field, type your server's URL. If you are using MadCap Feedback Service, type **madcap.**

5 In the **Feedback Service License Key** field, type your license key.

Viewing user comments

You can use the Feedback Explorer to review, accept, or delete user comments.

Shortcut	Toolbar	Menu
Alt+V, D	none	View > Feedback Explorer

To view user comments:

1 Open a topic.

2 Select **View > Feedback Explorer**.
The Feedback Explorer appears.

3 Select **Topic Comments** in the drop-down box at the top of the Feedback Explorer.

TIP ▷ *To save the comments to a Microsoft Excel .csv or .txt file, select the comments you want to save and select **File > Save To.***

Accepting or deleting user comments

You can accept or delete user comments. If you accept a comment, other users will be able to see the comment.

To accept or delete a comment:

1 Select **View > Feedback Explorer**.
   The Feedback Explorer appears.

2 Select **Pending Comments** in the drop-down box at the top of the Feedback Explorer.

3 Select a comment.

4 Do one of the following:

   □ To accept a comment, click the down arrow in the **Set comment status** field and select **Accepted**.

   □ To delete a comment, click 🗩.

5 Click **Yes**.

Viewing context-sensitive help calls

You can use the Feedback Explorer to track which topics have been opened using context-sensitive help.

To view context-sensitive help calls:

1 Select **View > Feedback Explorer**.
   The Feedback Explorer appears.

2 Select **Context-Sensitive Help Calls** in the drop-down box at the top of the Feedback Explorer.

Viewing users' search terms

You can use the Feedback Explorer to review user's search terms and search terms that did not match any topics.

To view user's search terms:

1 Select **View** > **Feedback Explorer**.
The Feedback Explorer appears.

2 Select **Search Phrases** or **Search Phrases with No Results** in
the drop-down box at the top of the Feedback Explorer.

Source control

You can add (or "bind") your project to any source control application that supports the Microsoft Source Code Control API (SCC API), including:

- Visual SourceSafe (VSS)
- Team Foundation Server (TFS)
- CVS
- Perforce
- Rational ClearCase
- Subversion

A source control application can prevent team members from overwriting each other's changes, save past versions of files, and identify changes made to files (and who made them).

Binding a project to source control

Flare provides built-in support for Visual SourceSafe (VSS) and Team Foundation Server (TFS), which means you can bind your project to VSS or TFS and then check in and check out files within Flare. For other source control applications, you will need a plug-in to integrate the application with Flare. Or, you can check out the files in your source control application, use Flare to makde changes, then check in the files outide of Flare.

Shortcut	Toolbar	Menu
Alt+P, J		Project > Project Properties

To bind a project to a source control application:

1   Select **Project** > **Project Properties**.
    The Project Properties dialog box appears.

2   Select the **Source Control** tab.

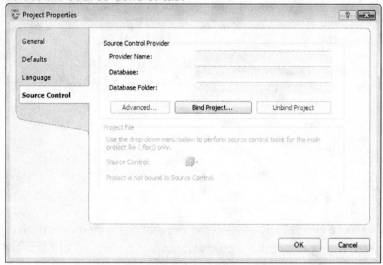

3   Click **Bind Project**.
    The Bind Project dialog box appears.

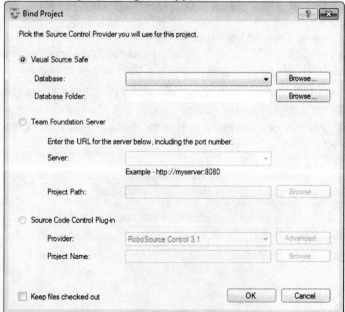

4 Select a **Source Control Provider** and provide the required information.

5 Select **Keep files checked out** if you want to keep the files checked out after they are added to the source control application.

6 Click **OK**.

Adding a file to source control

When you add a file to your project, you can also add it to your source control application. A ✦ plus sign icon will appear beside new files that have not been added to source control.

Shortcut	Toolbar	Menu
Alt+F, U, A	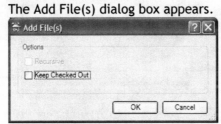	File > Source Control > Add

To add a file to source control:

1 Select a file or folder that is not in source control.

2 Right-click and select **Source Control > Add File**.
—OR—
Click ⬛ in the toolbar and select **Add File**.
The Add File(s) dialog box appears.

3 If you selected a folder, select **Recursive** if you want to add all of the files inside the folder.

4 If you want to keep editing the file, select **Keep Checked Out**.

5 Click **OK**.

Getting the latest version of a file

Before you make changes to a file, you should make sure you have the latest version from source control. A 🕒 clock icon will appear in the Content Explorer beside any local file that is older than the source control version.

Shortcut	Toolbar	Menu
Alt+F, U, G	📁	File > Source Control > Get Latest Version

To get the latest version of a file:

1 Select **File** > **Source Control** > **Project** > **Get Latest Version All**.

The Get Latest Version dialog box appears.

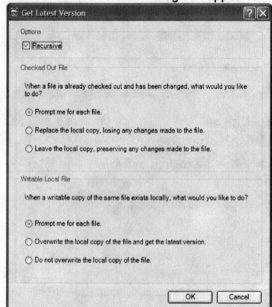

2 Select a **Checked Out File** option.

3 Select a **Writable Local File** option.

4 Click **OK**.

The latest version of the files are copied to your computer.

Checking out a file

You should check out a file before you modify it. When you check out a file, other users see a ♙ icon beside it in the Content Explorer.

If you do not check out a file, other users may modify it while you are making changes. See "Merging changes" for information about resolving your changes.

Shortcut	Toolbar	Menu
Alt+F, U, H		File > Source Control > Check Out

To check out a file:

1 Select a topic in the Content Explorer or File List.
 —OR—
 Select a project file in the Project Organizer.

2 Right-click and select **Source Control** > **Check Out**.
 —OR—
 Click in the toolbar and select **Check Out**.

The Check Out dialog box appears.

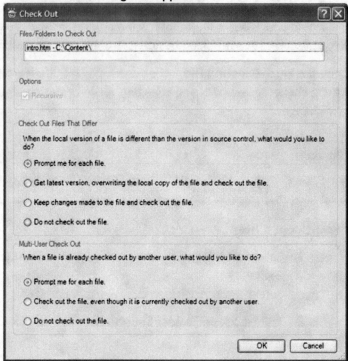

3 If you selected a folder, select **Recursive** if you want to add all of the files inside the folder.

4 Select a **Check Out Files That Differ** option.

5 Select a **Multi-User Check Out** option.

6 Click **OK**.

A ✓ checkmark icon appears beside the filename in the Content Explorer.

Checking in a file

After you have made changes to a file, you can check it in to source control so that other users can work with it.

Shortcut	Toolbar	Menu
Alt+F, U, C	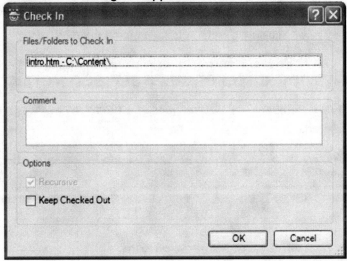	File > Source Control > Check In

To check in a file:

1 Select a topic in the Content Explorer or File List.
   —OR—
   Select a project file in the Project Organizer.

2 Right-click and select **Source Control** > **Check In**.
   —OR—
   Click [icon] in the toolbar and select **Check In**.
   The Check In dialog box appears.

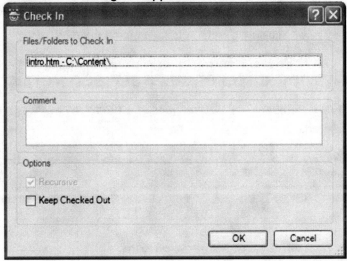

3 Type a check in **Comment**.

4 If you selected a folder, select **Recursive** if you want to add all of the files inside the folder.

5 Select **Keep Checked Out** if you want to check in the current version and keep editing the file.

6 Click **OK**.
A 🔒 lock appears beside the filename in the Content Explorer.

Viewing a list of checked out files

You can view a list of files that are checked out by you or other users.

Shortcut	Toolbar	Menu
Alt+F, U, D		File > Source Control > Pending Check-Ins

To view a list of files that are checked out:

1 Select **View** > **Pending Check-Ins**.
The Pending Check-Ins pane opens.

2 Scroll to the right to view the Status and User columns.

3 To sort the list, click a column heading.

Viewing differences between versions

You can compare any two versions of a file to review how a file has changed.

Shortcut	Toolbar	Menu
Alt+F, U, V		File > Source Control > View History

To view differences between versions:

1 Select a topic In the Content Explorer or File List.
—OR—
Select a project file in the Project Organizer.

2 Right-click and select **Source Control** > **View History**.
—OR—

Click 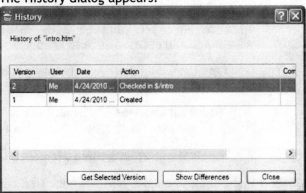 in the toolbar and select **View History**.
The History dialog box appears.

3 Select two versions of the file.

4 Click **Show Differences**.

Rolling back to a previous version

You can roll back to a previous checked in version of a file.

Shortcut	Toolbar	Menu
Alt+F, U, V		File > Source Control > View History

To roll back to a previous version:

1 Select a topic in the Content Explorer or File List.
—OR—

Select a project file in the Project Organizer.

2 Right-click and select **Source Control** > **View History**.
—OR—

Click in the toolbar and select **View History**.
The History dialog appears.

3 Select a version of the file.

4 Click **Get Selected Version**.
The selected version will be copied to the project.

5 Click **Close**.

Merging changes NEW!

If two users have modified a file at the same time, you can merge the changes and try to preserve both user's modifications.

Shortcut	Toolbar	Menu
Alt+F, U, C		File > Source Control > Check In

To merge changes:

1 Check in or get the latest version of a file.
If your version is different from the version in source control, the Resolve Conflicts dialog box appears.

2 Click **Auto Merge All**.
If the differences do not conflict, the versions are merged. If the differences conflict, complete the following steps.

3 Click **OK**.

4 Click **Resolve**.

5 Select a resolution option:

□ **Merge changes in merge tool** – Opens a merging interface, which lets you see exactly what changes were made and choose which to keep.

□ **Undo my local changes** – Automatically removes your changes and keeps changes from other authors.

□ **Discard server changes** – Automatically removes changes from other authors and keeps your changes.

6 If you selected **Merge changes in merge tool**, you can:

□ **Right-click** to open a context menu that can be used to keep or ignore a particular change to either the server or local version.

□ **Left-click** to keep the change to the server or local version.

□ **Type** content to edit the content and merge the versions yourself.

7 Click **OK** when all of the conflicts are resolved.

Sample questions for this section

1 Topic templates have the following extension:
A) htm
B) htt
C) temp
D) fltt

2 File tags can be applied to:
A) Only topics
B) topics and images
C) topics, images, videos, and sounds
D) any type of file in your project

3 You can create the reports based on the following information in Flare:
A) File tags
B) Used and unused styles, variables, and images
C) Both of the above
D) None of the above. You can only create reports in Analyzer.

4 Annotations...
A) True
B) False

5 Reviewers need to install Flare to review your topics.
A) True
B) False

6 Which source control applications have built-in support in Flare?
A) Any that support the MS SCC API
B) SVN and CVS
C) VSS and TFS
D) All of them

7 Why would you use MadCap Feedback?
A) To send bug reports.
B) To send information to MadCap if Flare crashes.
C) To add surveys to your project.
D) To allow users to rate and/or add comments to topics.

Appendices

This section covers:

- Additional resources
- Keyboard shortcuts
- Guide to Flare files
- Quick task index
- Answers to sample questions

Additional resources

Requesting new features

MadCap encourages users to request new features. You can request a feature by opening the Start Page (**View** > **Start Page**) and clicking 'Feature Requests.'

Reporting Flare bugs

MadCap Software does an excellent job of responding to customer problems and fixing bugs. Bug reports use the same form as feature requests. To submit a big report, open the Start Page (**View** > **Start Page**) and click 'Feature Requests.'

Flare discussion forums

You can use the Flare discussion forums to research Flare issues, post questions, and meet other Flare users. It's a very active and friendly community. You can visit the discussion groups by selecting **Help** > **Help Community** or by typing www.forums.madcapsoftware.com into a browser.

Keyboard shortcuts (by task)

Opening projects and topics

Shortcut	Description
Alt-F4	Close Flare
Ctrl+F4	Close the current window
F4	Open the Properties dialog box from the Content Explorer
Ctrl+O	Open a project
Ctrl+T	Create a new topic
Ctrl+Tab	Open a 'task switcher' popup displaying icons for all open windows. Pressing Ctrl-Tab again to move through the list.
Ctrl+Shift+Tab	After pressing Ctrl-Tab, move backward through open window list.
Ctrl+Shift+P	Open the Properties dialog box from within the XML Editor

Selecting text

Shortcut	Description
Ctrl+Left Arrow	Move the cursor to the next word to the left
Ctrl+Right Arrow	Move the cursor to the next word to the right
Ctrl+Shift+Left Arrow	Select the next word to the left
Ctrl+Shift+Right Arrow	Select the next word to the right
Ctrl+1	List matches (IntelliSense)
Ctrl+2	List frequent phrases (IntelliSense)

Shortcut	Description
Ctrl+3	List variables (IntelliSense)
Ctrl+A	Select all
Ctrl+C	Copy
Ctrl+V	Paste
Ctrl+X	Cut
Ctrl+Y	Redo
Ctrl+Z	Undo
Ctrl+Insert	Copy
Shift+Delete	Cut
Shift+Insert	Paste
Shift+Tab	Select the previous cell in a table
Del	Delete
Tab	Select the next cell in a table, or when you press Tab in the last row of a table, add a new row

Formatting text

Shortcut	Description
F12	Open the Style window
Ctrl+F12	Open the Local Formatting window
Ctrl+Alt+B	Open the Paragraph Properties dialog box
Ctrl+Shift+B	Open the Font Properties dialog box
Ctrl+Shift+H	Open the Style Picker
Shift+F12	Open the Attributes window

Shortcut	Description
Ctrl+B	Bold
Ctrl+I	Italic
Ctrl+U	Underline

Linking

Shortcut	Description
Ctrl+K	Insert a hyperlink
Ctrl+Shift+K	Insert a bookmark
Ctrl+Shift+R	Insert a cross reference
Ctrl+Shift+T	Insert a glossary term link
Shift+F9	Open the Concepts window

Saving

Shortcut	Description
Ctrl+S	Save
Alt+Ctrl+S	Save as
Ctrl+Shift+S	Save all

Spell checking

Shortcut	Description
F7	Open the Spell Check window

Working with the index and TOC

Shortcut	Description
F2	Highlight TOC entry for editing
F9	Open the Index window
F10	Insert the selected text as an index keyword
Ctrl+F8	Open the 'master' TOC

Searching

Shortcut	Description
F3	Find next
Alt+Ctrl+F	Open the Find in Files window
Ctrl+F	Open the Find and Replace window
Ctrl+G	Open the Find and Replace window with highlighted text in the 'Find what' field
Ctrl+Shift+F	Add the selected text to the 'Find what' field in the Find and Replace or Find in Files window

Opening and docking windows

Shortcut	Description
Ctrl+J	Open the Content Explorer
Ctrl+W	Open the Project Organizer
Ctrl+Shift+D	Move the active document to the Document Dock
Ctrl+Shift+I	Open the Instant Messages window

Shortcut	Description
Ctrl+Shift+J	Open the File List
Ctrl+Shift+O	Open the Messages window
Ctrl+Shift+W	Open the Start page

Publishing

Shortcut	Description
F6	Build the primary target
Ctrl+F6	Publish the primary target
Ctrl+F9	Open the primary target in Target Editor
Shift+F6	Open the primary target

Opening Flare's help system

Shortcut	Description
F1	Open a context-sensitive help topic
Alt-Ctrl+F1	Open the help system's TOC
Alt+F1	Open the help system's index
Alt+Shift+F2	Open the help system's index results window
Ctrl+F1	Open the help system's search
Ctrl+F3	Open a context-sensitive help topic in the dynamic help window

Keyboard shortcuts (by key)

Shortcut	Description
Alt+Ctrl+B	Open the Paragraph Properties dialog box
Alt+Ctrl+F	Open the Find in Files window
Alt+Ctrl+S	Save as
Alt-Ctrl+F1	Open the Flare help system's TOC
Alt+Shift+F2	Open the Flare help system's index results window
Alt+F1	Open the Flare help system's index
Alt+F4	Close Flare
Ctrl+F1	Open the Flare help system's search
Ctrl+F3	Open a context-sensitive help topic
Ctrl+F4	Close active window
Ctrl+F6	Publish the primary target
Ctrl+F8	Open the 'master' TOC
Ctrl+F9	Open Primary target in Target Editor
Ctrl+F12	Open the Local Formatting window
Ctrl+1	List matches (IntelliSense)
Ctrl+2	List frequent phrases (IntelliSense)
Ctrl+3	List variables (IntelliSense)
Ctrl+A	Select all
Ctrl+B	Bold
Ctrl+C	Copy
Ctrl+F	Open the Find and Replace window
Ctrl+G	Open the Find and Replace window with highlighted text in 'Find what' field

Shortcut	Description
Ctrl+I	Italic
Ctrl+J	Opens the Content Explorer
Ctrl+K	Insert a hyperlink
Ctrl+O	Open a new project
Ctrl+P	Print
Ctrl+S	Save
Ctrl+T	Create a new topic
Ctrl+U	Underline
Ctrl+V	Paste
Ctrl+W	Open the Project Organizer
Ctrl+X	Cut
Ctrl+Y	Redo
Ctrl+Z	Undo
Ctrl+Insert	Copy
Ctrl+Left Arrow	Move the insertion point cursor to the next word to the left
Ctrl+Right Arrow	Move the insertion point cursor to the next word to the right
Ctrl+Shift+B	Open the Font Properties dialog box
Ctrl+Shift+D	Move the active document to the Document Dock
Ctrl+Shift+F	Add the selected text to the 'Find what' field in the Find and Replace or Find in Files window
Ctrl+Shift+H	Open the Style Picker
Ctrl+Shift+I	Open the Instant Messages window
Ctrl+Shift+J	Open the File List
Ctrl+Shift+K	Insert a bookmark
Ctrl+Shift+O	Open the Messages window
Ctrl+Shift+P	Open the Properties dialog box from within the XML Editor

Shortcut	Description
Ctrl+Shift+R	Insert a cross reference
Ctrl+Shift+S	Save all
Ctrl+Shift+T	Insert a glossary term link
Ctrl+Shift+W	Open the Start page
Ctrl+Shift+Left Arrow	Select the next word to the left
Ctrl+Shift+Right Arrow	Select the next word to the right
Ctrl+Shift+Tab	After pressing Ctrl-Tab, move backward through open window list.
Ctrl+Tab	Open a 'task switcher' popup displaying icons for all open windows. Pressing Ctrl-Tab again to move through the list.
Del	Delete
F1	Open a context-sensitive help topic
F2	Highlight for editing
F3	Find next
F4	Open the Properties dialog box from the Content Explorer
F5	Refresh
F6	Build the primary target
F7	Open the Spell Check window
F9	Open the Index window
F10	Insert the selected text as an index keyword
F11	Insert quick character
F12	Open the Style window
Shift+Delete	Cut
Shift+F6	Open the primary target
Shift+F9	Open the Concepts window
Shift+F12	Open the Attributes window

Shortcut	Description
Shift+Insert	Paste
Shift+Space	Insert non-breaking space
Shift+Tab	Select the previous cell in a table
Tab	Select the next cell in a table, or, if you press Tab in the last row of a table, add a new row

Guide to Flare files

The following table lists all of the file types that are used in Flare, their extension, and their default folder.

File Type	Extension	Default Folder
Analyzer database	fldb	Analyzer\Content.cadbf
Batch target	flbat	Project\Targets
Browse sequence	flbrs	Project\Advanced
Condition tag set	flcts	Project\ConditionTagSets
Context-sensitive help alias file	flali	Project\Advanced
Context-sensitive help header file	h or hh	Project\Advanced
Dependency set	fllnks	Output\Temporary
Dictionary	tlx	Program Files\MadCap Software\MadCap Flare *V6*\Flare.app\Resources\SSCE
DITA topic	dita	Output*name of DITA target*
DITA map	ditamap	Output*name of DITA target*
DITA import template	flimpdita	Project\Imports
DotNet Help entry file	mchelp	Output*name of DotNet Help target*
File tag set	flfts	Project\Advanced
FrameMaker import template	flimpfm	Project\Imports
Glossary	flglo	Project\Glossaries
HTML Help	chm	Output*name of HTML Help target*

File Type	Extension	Default Folder
Image	bmp, emf, exps, gif, hdp, jpg, png, tif, wdp, wmf, xaml, xps	**New projects:** Content\Resources\Images **Imported projects:** Content
Index auto-index phrase set	flaix	Project\Advanced
Index link set	flixl	Project\Advanced
Language skin	fllng	Program Files\MadCap Software\MadCap Flare *V6*\Flare.app\Resources\LanguageSkins
Master page	flmsp	Content\Resources\MasterPages
Page layout	flpgl	Content\Resources\PageLayouts
PDF file	pdf	Output*name of PDF target*
Project file	flprj	top-level folder
Project import template	flimpfl	Project\Imports
Publishing destination	fldes	Project\Destinations
Relationship table	flrtb	Project\Advanced
Report	flrep	Project\Reports
Reviewed topic	fltrev	Content
Search filter set	flsfs	Project\Advanced
Search synonyms	mcsyns	Project\Advanced
Skin	flskn	Project\Skins
Snippet	flsnp	Content\Resources\Snippets
Sound	mid, mpa, mp3, mp4, wav, wma	**New projects:** Content\Resources\Multimedia **Imported projects:** Content

File Type	Extension	Default Folder
Stylesheet	css	**New projects:** Content\Resources\Stylesheets **Imported projects:** Content
Table stylesheet	css	Content\Resources\TableStyles
Target	fltar	Project\Targets
Target build error log	mclog	Project\Reports
TOC	fltoc	Project\TOCs
Topic (generated)	htm	Output
Topic (source)	htm	Content
Variable set	flvar	Project\VariableSets
Video	mov, mpg, qt, wmv, swf	**New projects:** Content\Resources\Multimedia **Imported projects:** Content
WebHelp AIR entry file	air	Output*name of WebHelp AIR target*
Window layout	panellayout	Documents and Settings\ Application Data\MadCap Software
Word import template	flimp	Project\Imports
XHTML document	xhtml	Output*name of XHTML target*
XPS document	xps	Output*name of XPS target*

Quick task index

The quick task index provides the basic steps for every major task you can perform in Flare.

Projects

Task	Steps	See Page
Creating a project	1 Select **File > New Project**.	22
	2 Type a **Project Name** and **Project Folder** and click **Next**.	
	3 Select a **Language** and click **Next**.	
	4 Select a **Template Folder** and **Template** and click **Next**.	
	5 Select an **Available Target** and click **Next**.	
	6 Select **Create the Project** and click **Finish**.	
Importing a RoboHelp project	1 Select **File > Import Project > Import (Non-Flare) Project**.	35
	2 Click ⬚, locate and select a project, and click **Open**.	
	3 Click **Next**.	
	4 Type a **Project Name**, select a **Project Folder**, and click **Next**.	
	5 Select whether you want to **Convert all topics at once** and/or to **Convert inline formatting to CSS styles** and click **Next**.	
	6 Select a language for the spell checker and click **Next**.	
	7 Click **Finish**.	
Creating a project based on a FrameMaker document	1 Select **File > Import Project > Import FrameMaker Documents**.	36
	2 Click **Next**.	
	3 Click **Add Files**, select a file, and click **Open**.	
	4 Select whether you want to link to the original FrameMaker document and click **Next**.	
	5 Type a **Project Name**, type or select a **Project Folder**, and click **Next**.	
	6 Select a style or styles to use to create new topics and click **Next**.	
	7 Select whether you want to create new topics based on the length of your Word document and click **Next**.	
	8 Select a stylesheet and click **Next**.	
	9 Map your styles and click **Next**.	
	10 Click **Finish**.	

Task	Steps	See Page
Creating a project based on a Word document	1 Select **File > Import Project > Import Word Documents**.	55
	2 Click **Next**.	
	3 Click **Add Files**, select a file, and click **Open**.	
	4 Select whether you want to link to the original Word document and click **Next**.	
	5 Type a **Project Name**, type or select a **Project Folder**, and click **Next**.	
	6 Select a style or styles to use to create new topics and click **Next**.	
	7 Select whether you want to create new topics based on the length of your Word document and click **Next**.	
	8 Select a stylesheet and click **Next**.	
	9 Map your styles and click **Next**.	
	10 Click **Finish**.	
Importing a DITA document set	1 Select **File > Import Project > Import DITA Document Set**.	61
	2 Click **Next**.	
	3 Click **Add Files**.	
	4 Select a .dita or .ditamap file and click **Open**.	
	5 If you plan to continue editing the original DITA files, select **Link generated files to source files**.	
	6 Click **Next**.	
	7 Type a **Project Name**.	
	8 Type or select a **Project Folder** and Click **Next**.	
	9 Select **Import all content files to one folder** if you want to import all of the DITA documents into one folder.	
	10 Select **'Auto-reimport before Generate Output'** if you want to automatically re-import the DITA document(s) when you generate a target.	
	11 Select **Preserve ID attributes for elements** if you plan to build a DITA target from your project.	
	12 Click **Next**.	
	13 Click **Conversion Styles** if you want to change	

	the formatting of your topics.	
	14 Select a stylesheet for the new topic(s).	
	15 Click **Finish**.	

Topics

Task	Steps	See Page
Creating a topic	1 Select **Project** > **Add Topic**.	47
	2 Select a **Source** template.	
	3 Type a **File Name**.	
	4 Select a **Stylesheet**.	
	5 Click **Add** and click **OK**.	
Importing a FrameMaker document	1 Create or open a FrameMaker import file.	35
	2 Click **Add Files**.	
	3 Select a FrameMaker document and click **Open**.	
	4 Select whether you want to link the generated files to the source files.	
	5 Select the **New Topic Styles** tab and select the styles to use to create new topics.	
	6 Select the **Options** tab and select whether you want to create new topics based on the length of your Word document.	
	7 Select the **Stylesheet** tab and select a stylesheet.	
	8 Select the **Paragraph Styles** tab and map your paragraph styles.	
	9 Select the **Character Styles** tab and map your character styles.	
	10 Select the **Cross Reference Styles** tab and map your cross-reference (x-ref) styles.	
	11 Click **Import** and click **Accept**.	
Importing a Word document	1 Create or open an MS Word import file.	55
	2 Click **Add Files**.	
	3 Select a Word document and click **Open**.	
	4 Select whether you want to link the generated files to the source files.	

Task	Steps	See Page
	5 Select the **New Topic Styles** tab and select the styles to use to create new topics.	
	6 Select the **Options** tab and select whether you want to create new topics based on the length of your Word document.	
	7 Select the **Stylesheet** tab and select a stylesheet.	
	8 Select the **Paragraph Styles** tab and map your paragraph styles.	
	9 Select the **Character Styles** tab and map your character styles.	
	10 Click **Import** and click **Accept**.	
Importing a DITA file	1 Create or open a DITA import file.	61
	2 Click **Add Files**.	
	3 Select a .dita or .ditamap file and click **Open**.	
	4 Select whether you want to link the generated files to the source files.	
	5 Select the **Options** tab and select whether you want to import your content into one folder.	
	6 Select the **Stylesheet** tab and select a stylesheet.	
	7 Click **Import** and click **Accept**.	
Importing an HTML file	1 Select **Project > Import HTML Files**.	66
	2 Click **Add Files**.	
	3 Select a .htm, .html, or .xhtml document and click **Open**.	
	4 Click **Next**.	
	5 Select a folder for the imported topics.	
	6 Select **Import resources** if you also want to import any files that are used by the selected document(s).	
	7 Click **Finish**.	
Importing content from Flare projects	1 Create or open a Flare project import file.	66
	2 Click **Browse**.	
	3 Select a Flare project file and click **Open**.	
	4 Select whether you want to automatically re-import the files when you build a target.	
	5 For **Include Files**, select the files or file types	

Task	Steps	See Page
	to be linked.	
	6 For **Exclude Files**, select the file types to not be linked.	
	7 Click **Import**.	

Topic content

Task	Steps	See Page
Inserting a special character	1 Select **Insert > Character**. 2 Select a character.	52
Creating a list	1 Click the down arrow to the right of the ☰ icon in the Text format toolbar. 2 Select a list type. 3 Type the list items.	71
Sorting a list	1 Select the list. 2 Click ▦ to view the block bars. 3 Click the list's ol or ul tag. 4 Select **Sort List**.	72
Inserting a table	1 Select **Table > Insert > Table**. 2 Select a number of columns and rows. 3 Select a number of header and footer rows. 4 Type a table caption and select a caption location. 5 Select a column width. 6 Click **OK**.	73
Creating a table style	1 Select **Project > Add Table Style**. 2 Select a **Source** template. 3 Select a **Folder**. 4 Type a **File Name**. 5 Click **Add** and click **OK**.	75
Assigning a table style to a table	1 Click inside a table. 2 Select **Table > Table Properties**. 3 Select a **Table Style**.	79

Task	Steps	See Page
	4 Click **OK.**	
Inserting an image	1 Select **Insert > Picture.**	82
	2 Click **Browse**, select an image, and click **Open.**	
	3 Type a **Screen Tip.**	
	4 Click **OK.**	
Inserting a sound or video	1 Select **Insert > Multimedia >** and either **Flash Movie, Windows Media Player**, or **Quicktime Movie.**	84, 85
	2 Click **Browse**, select a sound or video file, and click **Open.**	
	3 Type a **Screen Tip.**	
	4 Click **OK.**	

Links

Task	Steps	See Page
Creating a link	1 Select the text or image that you want to use as the link.	91
	2 Select **Insert > Hyperlink.**	
	3 Select the type of link you want to create.	
	4 Select a link target (a topic, file, or website).	
	5 Select a **Target Frame.**	
	6 Type a **Screen Tip.**	
	7 Click **OK.**	
Creating an image map link	1 Select the image to which you want to add links and select **Image Map.**	96
	2 Select an image map shape and draw the image map area.	
	3 Select a link target type and target.	
	4 Select a **Target Frame.**	
	5 Type a **Screen Tip.**	
	6 Click **OK.**	
Creating a topic popup	1 Select the text or image that you want to use as the link.	98
	2 Select **Insert > Topic Popup.**	
	3 Select the type of link you want to create.	

Task	Steps		See Page
	4	Select a link target (a topic, file, or website).	
	5	Select **Popup Window** as the **Target Frame**.	
	6	Type a **Screen Tip**.	
	7	Click **OK**.	
Creating a text popup	1	Select the text or image that you want to use as the link.	100
	2	Select **Insert > Popup**.	
	3	Type the popup text.	
	4	Click **OK**.	
Creating a cross reference	1	Position your cursor where you want to add the cross reference.	101
	2	Select **Insert > Cross Reference**.	
	3	For **Link To**, select **Topic in Project**.	
	4	Select a topic.	
	5	Click **OK**.	
Finding and fixing broken links	1	Select **View > Project Analysis**.	97
	2	Select **Broken Links**.	
	3	Double-click a broken link in the list.	
	4	Right-click the highlighted link and select **Edit Hyperlink**.	
	5	Select a new link location.	
	6	Click **OK**.	

Drop-down, expanding, and toggler links

Task	Steps		See Page
Creating a drop-down link	1	Open the topic that will contain the link.	103
	2	Highlight the drop-down link and drop-down text.	
	3	Select **Insert > Drop-Down Text**.	
	4	Highlight the drop-down link (or 'head').	
	5	Click **OK**.	
Creating an expanding link	1	Open the topic that will contain the link.	104
	2	Highlight the expanding link and expanding	

Task	Steps	See Page
	text.	
	3 Select **Insert** > **Expanding Text**.	
	4 Highlight the expanding link (or 'hotspot').	
	5 Click **OK**.	
Creating a toggler link	1 Click the tag bar next to the content that you want to show and hide.	105
	2 In the popup menu, select **Name**.	
	3 Type a name for the element and click **OK**.	
	4 Highlight the text that you want to use as the toggler hotspot.	
	5 Select **Insert** > **Toggler**.	
	6 Select a toggler target.	
	7 Click **OK**.	

Related topic, keyword, and concept links

Task	Steps	See Page
Creating a related topics link	1 Select **Insert** > **Help Control** > **Related Topics Control**.	108
	2 Select a topic to add to the link.	
	3 Click ⸌⸜⸜⸜⸝ to add the topic to the related topics link.	
	4 Add more topics as needed.	
	5 Click **OK**.	
Creating a keyword link	1 Select **Insert** > **Help Control** > **Keyword Link Control**.	109
	2 Select a keyword.	
	3 Click ⸌⸜⸜⸜⸝ to add the keyword to the keyword link.	
	4 Add more keywords as needed.	
	5 Click **OK**.	
Creating a concept link	1 Add a concept group.	110
	2 Open a topic to associate with the concept group.	
	3 Select **Tools** > **Concepts** > **Concepts Window**.	

Task	Steps	See Page
	4 Type a term and press **Enter**.	
	5 Click **Save**.	
	6 Select **Insert** > **Help Control** > **Concept Link**.	
	7 Select a concept.	
	8 Click ⌧ to add the concept to the concept link.	
	9 Click **OK**.	

Relationship links

Task	Steps	See Page
Creating a relationship table	1 Select **Project** > **Advanced** > **Add Relationship Table**. 2 Select a **Template Folder** and **Template**. 3 Type a **File Name**. 4 Click **Add**.	113
Adding a relationship to a relationship table	1 Open a relationship table. 2 Click 🖹 to create a new row. 3 Click 🖉. 4 Type a name for the row. 5 Click **OK**. 6 Click a cell. 7 Click 🖹. 8 Select a topic and click **OK**.	114
Creating a relationship link	1 Select **Insert** > **Proxy** > **Insert Relationships Proxy**. 2 Click **OK**.	117

Navigational tools

Task	Steps	See Page
Creating a TOC book	1 Click 🖻.	125
	2 Click 🗋 in the TOC Editor toolbar.	
	3 Press **F2**.	
	4 Type a name.	
Creating a TOC page	1 Click 🖻.	125
	2 Double-click the TOC page.	
	3 Type a **Label** for the page.	
	4 Click **Select Link**.	
	5 Select a topic.	
	6 Click **Open**.	
	7 Click **OK**.	
Finding and fixing issues in a TOC	1 If your TOC books are intentionally unlinked, click 🖻.	126
	2 Click 🖻.	
	3 Right-click the TOC item and select **Properties**.	
	4 On the **General** tab, select a new link and click **OK**.	
Finding topics that are not in a TOC	1 Select **View > Project Analysis**.	132
	2 Select **Topics Not In Selected TOC**.	
	3 For **Filter**, select a TOC.	
Creating an index entry	1 Click before or on the word or phrase that you want to insert as an index entry.	133
	2 Press **F9**.	
	3 Type a term and press **Enter**.	
Finding topics that are not in the index	1 Select **View > Project Analysis**.	138
	2 Select **Topics Not In Index**.	
Excluding a topic from	1 Right-click a topic and select **Properties**.	141
	2 Select the **Topic Properties** tab.	

Task	Steps	See Page
the search	3 Deselect the **Include topic when full-text search database is generated** option.	
	4 Click **OK**.	
Creating a glossary entry and link	1 Highlight the word or phrase that will become the glossary link.	142
	2 Select **Insert > Glossary Term Link**.	
	3 Select a **Glossary File**.	
	4 Type a definition.	
	5 Click **OK**.	
Creating a browse sequence	1 Select **Project > Advanced > Add Browse Sequence**.	146
	2 Select a **Source** template.	
	3 Type a **File Name**.	
	4 Click **Add** and Click **OK**.	

Formatting and layout

Task	Steps	See Page
Creating a stylesheet	1 Select **Project > Add Stylesheet**.	158
	2 Select a **Source** template.	
	3 Select a **Folder**.	
	4 Type a **File Name**.	
	5 Click **Add** and click **OK**.	
Creating a style	1 Use the **Format** menu commands to format the text.	161
	2 Click inside the formatted content. Do not highlight the content.	
	3 Select **View > Style Window**.	
	4 Click **Create Style**.	
	5 Type a name for the new style.	
	6 Select whether the style should be applied to the highlighted content.	
	7 Click **OK**.	
Creating a master page	1 Select **Project > Add Master Page**.	171
	2 Select a **Source** template.	

Task	Steps	See Page
	3 Type a file name for the master page.	
	4 Select a stylesheet.	
	5 Click **Add** and click **OK**.	
Creating a page layout	1 Select **Project > Add Page Layout.**	175
	2 Select a **Source** template.	
	3 Type a file name for the page layout.	
	4 Click **Add** and click **OK.**	
Creating a skin	1 Select **Project > Add Skin.**	180
	2 Select a **Source** template.	
	3 Type a file name for the skin.	
	4 Click **Add.**	
	5 Modify the skin options as needed.	

Variables and snippets

Task	Steps	See Page
Creating a variable	1 Click 🔲 in the Variable Set Editor toolbar.	194
	2 Type a name for the variable.	
	3 Type a definition for the variable.	
Inserting a variable	1 Select **Insert > Variable.**	195
	2 Select a variable set.	
	3 Select a variable.	
	4 Click **OK.**	
Creating a snippet from existing content	1 Highlight the content you want to convert to a snippet.	197
	2 Select **Format > Create Snippet.**	
	3 Type a name for the snippet.	
	4 Select **Replace Source Content with the New Snippet.**	
	5 Click **Create.**	
Creating a snippet from new content	1 Select **Project > Add Snippet.**	198
	2 Select a **Source** template.	

Task	Steps	See Page
	3 Type a **File Name**.	
	4 Click **Add** and click **OK**.	
Inserting a snippet	1 Select **Insert > Snippet**.	199
	2 Select a **Snippet Source**.	
	3 Select a snippet.	
	4 Click **OK**.	

Condition tags

Task	Steps	See Page
Creating a condition tag	1 Open a condition tag set.	202
	2 Click ⬚ in the Condition Tag Set Editor toolbar.	
	3 Press **F2**.	
	4 Type a new name for the tag and press **Enter**.	
	5 Select a color.	
Applying a condition tag to content	1 Select the content to be tagged.	203
	2 Select **Format > Conditions**.	
	3 Select a condition tag's checkbox.	
	4 Click **OK**.	
Applying a condition tag to a topic, file, or folder	1 Select the topic, file, or folder to be tagged.	203
	2 Click ⬚ in the Content Explorer toolbar.	
	3 Select the **Conditional Text** tab.	
	4 Select a condition tag's checkbox.	
	5 Click **OK**.	
Applying a condition tag to a TOC book or page	1 Open the TOC.	205
	2 Select a book or page and click ⬚.	
	3 Select the **Conditional Text** tab.	
	4 Select a condition tag's checkbox.	
	5 Click **OK**.	

Targets

Task	Steps	See Page
Creating a target	1 Select Project > **Add Target**. 2 Select a **Source** template. 3 Type a file name. 4 Click **Add**. 5 Click **Save**. 6 Set the target options as needed.	213
Building a target	▫ Right-click a target and select **Build**.	220
Viewing a target	▫ Right-click a target and select **View**.	221
Creating a publishing destination	1 Open a target. 2 Select **Project** > **Add Destination**. 3 Select a template folder and template. 4 Type a file name. 5 Click **Add**. 6 Select a target type. 7 Select a publishing location.	224
Publishing a target	1 Open a target. 2 Click ⬚. 3 Select one (or more) of the publishing destinations. 4 Click **Start Publishing**.	224
Batch generating targets	1 Create and open a batch target. 2 Select the **Schedule** tab. 3 Click **New**. 4 Select a frequency **Setting**. 5 Select a **Start** date and time. 6 If you selected a daily, weekly, or monthly frequency setting, select the recurrence details. 7 If the batch generate should repeat, select **Repeat task every** and specify how often and how long the repeating should occur.	221

Task	Steps	See Page
	8 If the repeating should expire, select **Expire** and specify an expiration date.	
	9 If you are ready to enable the batch generate, select **Enable**.	
	10 Click **OK**.	

Context-sensitive help

Task	Steps	See Page
Creating a header file	1 Select **Project > Advanced > Add Header File**. 2 Select a **Source** template. 3 Type a **File Name**. 4 Click **Add**.	230
Creating an alias file	1 Select **Project > Advanced > Add Alias File**. 2 Select a **Template Folder** and **Template**. 3 Type a **File Name**. 4 Click **Add**.	230
Assigning an identifier to a topic	1 Open an alias file. 2 Select an **Identifier**. 3 Select a **Topic**. 4 Select a **Skin** (optional). 5 Click **Assign**.	231
Testing context-sensitive help	1 Build your target. 2 Right-click the target in the Targets folder and select **Test CSH API Calls**. 3 Next to each identifier, click **Test**.	231

File tags and reports

Task	Steps	See Page
Creating a file tag set	1 Select **Project** > **Advanced** > **Add File Tag Set**. 2 Select a **Source** template. 3 Type a **File Name**. 4 Click **Add**.	238
Adding a tag	1 Open a file tag set. 2 Click 🗋. 3 Type a name for the tag.	239
Applying a tag	1 Right-click a file and select **Propeprties**. 2 Select the **File Tag** tab. 3 Select a **Tag Type**. 4 Select a **File Tag**. 5 Click **OK**.	239
Creating a report file	1 Select **Project** > **Add Report File**. 2 Select a **Source** template. 3 Type a **File Name**. 4 Click **Add**.	241
Generating a report	1 Open a report. 2 On the **General** tab, type a **Title** for the report. 3 Select the **Tables** to include in the report. 4 Click **Generate**.	242

Annotation and topic reviews

Task	Steps	See Page
Adding an annotation	1 Select the content you want to annotate. 2 Select **Insert** > **Insert Annotation**. 3 If this is your first annotation, type your initials. 4 Type your annotation.	243

Task	Steps	See Page
Locking content	1 Position your cursor inside the content you want to lock.	244
	2 Select **Format > Locks > Mark Element(s) to be Locked**.	
	3 Select **Format > Locks > Locks (Disabled)**.	
Sending a topic for review	1 Select **View > Toolbars > Review**.	244
	2 Click Send For Review... .	
	3 Type a **Review Package Name**.	
	4 Select the topics you want to send for review and click **Open**.	
	5 If you want to allow reviewers to edit the topic, select **Allow reviewers to edit content**.	
	6 Click **Next**.	
	7 Type a subject and message for the email.	
	8 Select a recipient.	
	9 Click **Send**.	
Accepting an annotation	1 Select **File > Review > Topic Reviews**.	245
	2 Select **Inbox**.	
	3 Select a topic.	
	4 Click Accept Annotations... .	
	5 Select the annotation(s) you want to accept.	
	6 Click **OK**.	
Accepting a reviewed topic	1 Select **File > Review > Topic Reviews**.	245
	2 Select **Inbox**.	
	3 Select a topic.	
	4 Click Accept Topic... .	
	5 Click **OK**.	

Feedback

Task	Steps	See Page
Enabling comments	1 Open a skin.	247
	2 Select the **General** tab.	

Task	Steps	See Page
	3 Select **Topic Comments.**	
	4 If you want to display the topic comments at the bottom of your topics, select **Display topic comments at the end of each topic.**	
Viewing comments	1 Select **View > Feedback Explorer.**	248
	2 Select **Topic Comments** in the drop-down box at the top of the Feedback Explorer.	
Accepting comments	1 Select **View > Feedback Explorer.**	249
	2 Select **Pending Comments** in the drop-down box at the top of the Feedback Explorer.	
	3 Select a comment.	
	4 Click the down arrow in the **Set comment status** field and select **Accepted.**	
	5 Click **Yes.**	
Viewing context-sensitive help calls	1 Select **View > Feedback Explorer.**	249
	2 Select **Context-Sensitive Help Calls** in the drop-down box at the top of the Feedback Explorer.	
Viewing search terms	1 Select **View > Feedback Explorer.**	249
	2 Select **Search Phrases** or **Search Phrases with No Results** in the drop-down box at the top of the Feedback Explorer.	

Source control

Task	Steps	See Page
Biding a project	1 Select **Project > Project Properties.**	251
	2 Select the **Source Control** tab.	
	3 Click **Bind Project.**	
	4 Select a **Source Control Provider** and provide the required information.	
	5 Select **Keep files checked out** if you want to keep the files checked out after they are added to the source control application.	
	6 Click **OK.**	
Adding a file	1 Select a file or folder that is not in source control.	253

Task	Steps	See Page
	2 Right-click and select **Source Control** > **Add File.**	
	3 If you selected a folder, select **Recursive** if you want to add all of the files inside the folder.	
	4 If you want to keep editing the file, select **Keep Checked Out.**	
	5 Click **OK.**	
Getting the latest version	1 Select **File** > **Source Control** > **Project** > **Get Latest Version All.**	254
	2 Select a **Checked Out File** option.	
	3 Select a **Writable Local File** option.	
	4 Click **OK.**	
Checking out a file	1 Select a topic in the Content Explorer or File List.	255
	2 Right-click and select **Source Control** > **Check Out.**	
	3 If you selected a folder, select **Recursive** if you want to add all of the files inside the folder.	
	4 Select a **Check Out Files That Differ** option.	
	5 Select a **Multi-User Check Out** option.	
	6 Click **OK.**	
Checking in a file	1 Select a topic In the Content Explorer or File List.	257
	2 Right-click and select **Source Control** > **Check In.**	
	3 Type a check in **Comment.**	
	4 If you selected a folder, select **Recursive** if you want to add all of the files inside the folder.	
	5 Select **Keep Checked Out** if you want to check in the current version and keep editing the file.	
	6 Click **OK.**	
Viewing a list of checked out files	1 Select **View** > **Pending Check-Ins.**	258
	2 Scroll to the right to view the Status and User columns.	

Task	Steps	See Page
Viewing differences	1 Select a topic In the Content Explorer or File List.	258
	2 Right-click and select **Source Control** > **View History**.	
	3 Select two versions of the file.	
	4 Click **Show Differences**.	
Rolling back	1 Select a topic in the Content Explorer or File List.	259
	2 Right-click and select **Source Control** > **View History**.	
	3 Select a version of the file.	
	4 Click **Get Selected Version**.	
Merging changes	1 Check in or get the latest version of a file.	260
	2 Click **Auto Merge All**.	
	3 Click **OK**.	
	4 Click **Resolve**.	
	5 Select a resolution option.	

Answers

Projects

Topics

Answers		
1	C	XHTML is an XML scheme and is the successor to HTML.
2	D	You can have as many topics open as you want.
3	C	You can link any Flare file between projects, including topics, stylesheets, and variables.
4	B	To import a PDF file, you should save it as an HTML and import the HTML file.
5	C	Table styles are table-specific stylesheets, and they have the CSS extension.
6	A	You can import jpg images (and many other types) into Flare. However, you cannot import svg, eps, or ai files into Flare 4.
7	B	To view a list of topics that contain an image, right-click the image in the Content Explorer and select **Show Dependencies.**

Links

		Answers
1	B	To view a list of topics that link to a topic, right-click the topic in the Content Explorer and select **Show Dependencies**.
2	C	To find and fix broken links, open the Project Analyzer tab and select the **Link** report.
3	D	An image map is an image that contains links.
4	B	You can set a cross reference's link label and formatting using the MadCap|xref style in your stylesheet.
5	A and B	Hyperlinks and popups can open a web page.
6	D	Drop-down and toggler links can show and hide content below the link. Expanding links always show and hide content in the same paragraph immediately *after* the link.
7	D	Keyword links will not work in the preview. Flare only adds the code for keyword links when you build a target.

Navigation

Answers

1   C   TOC files are stored in the Project Organizer's TOCs folder.

2   A   TOC pages do not have to be inside books.

3   C   You can add second-level index entries using a colon.

4   D   You can select View > Index Explorer to view your index keywords. Index keywords are stored in your topics, not in an index file.

5   B   To exclude a topic from the search, open the Topic Properties dialog box and deselect the **Include topic when full-text search database is generated** option.

6   C   In HTML Help, the glossary appears at the bottom of your table of contents. It appears as an accordion in WebHelp.

7   B   A browse sequence is an ordered list of links that can be used to find and open topics, like a TOC.

Formatting and design

Answers		
1	B	Inline formatting is applied by highlighting content and changing its appearance.
2	C	You should consider using a font set for WebHelp if your users are using different operating systems.
3	D	A master stylesheet is assigned to all topics.
4	A	The breadcrumb is the path to the current topic using the TOC.
5	D	You can create odd and even pages in a page layout to specify different footers in a print target.
6	C	The additional items will appear as icons below the accordion.
7	B	To select a skin, open the target and select the skin in the General tab.

Single sourcing

Answers		
1	A	Variables are stored in variable sets in the Project Organizer.
2	B and C	A variable's definition can be set in the VariableSet Editor and in a target on the Variables tab.
3	all	Snippets can contain formatted text, tables, lists, and variables.
4	B	Snippets are stored in snippet files in the Content Explorer.
5	All	Condition tags can be applied to topics, folders, TOC books and pages, and index keywords.
6	D	You must reapply to tag to your content using the new tag name.
7	All	Condition tags can be used with any target type.

Publishing

1	A and C	MadCap Softwre created the DotNet Help and WebHelp formats. The HTML Help and XPS formats were created by Microsoft.
2	C	The 'Mark of the Web' option will turn off the 'Active Content' message when you open WebHelp locally from your PC.
3	A	A primary target is the main target you plan to create in your project, and it sets the target that is used for the preview. However, you can create any target type from your project.
4	D	You can set up as many target as you need for your project.
5	C	Flare deletes everything in the Output folder when you select Build > Clean project.
6	B	Flare copies your files to a network or website when you publish a target.
7	B	The "startup" topic is the first topic users see when they open an online target.

Project management

Answers		
1	A	Topic templates use the same extension as topics: htm.
2	D	File tags can be applied to any type of file, including topics, images, videos, sounds, master pages, page layouts, skins, and stylesheets.
3	C	You can create reports based on file tags and/or unused or used styles, variables, and images.
4	B	Annotations are not included when you build a target.
5	B	Reviewers can use the free X-Edit application to review topics. They do not need to install Flare.
6	C	Flare provides built-in support for VSS and TFS.
7	D	Feedback can be used to allow users to rate and/or add comments to topics.

Index

CSS to the Point

CSS to the Point provides focused answers to over 150 cascading stylesheet (CSS) questions. Each answer includes a description of the solution, a graphical example, and sample code that has been tested in Internet Explorer, Firefox, Opera and Safari. If you have been struggling with CSS, this book will help you use CSS like a pro.

You can order *CSS to the Point* at **www.lulu.com/clickstart**.

Training

ClickStart offers training for Flare, Blaze, Captivate, and CSS. Our training classes extend what you have learned in this book with practice exercises, best practices, and advanced challenges.

We teach online and onsite classes (worldwide), and we offer group discounts for 4 or more students. For more information, visit our website at **www.clickstart.net** or email us at **info@clickstart.net**.

Consulting

ClickStart also offers a full range of consulting and contracting services, including:

- Migrating RoboHelp, Word, and FrameMaker projects to Flare
- Developing best practices for creating online help, user guides, and policies and procedures
- Improving workflow and increasing efficiency
- Single sourcing content for multiple audiences
- Designing stylesheets, page layouts, master pages, skins, and style guides
- Developing context-sensitive help and embedded user assistance

For more information, visit our website at **www.clickstart.net** or email us at **info@clickstart.net**.

9 780578 001173